The Student's Music Library
Historical and Critical Studies
Edited by Percy M. Young, M.A., Mus. D.

SCHUBERT'S PIANO WORKS

SCHUBERT'S PIANO WORKS

Ernest G. Porter

LONDON: DENNIS DOBSON

© 1980 by Ernest G. Porter
First published in Great Britain in 1980 by
Dobson Books Ltd, 80 Kensington Church Street,
London W8 4BZ

Printed in Great Britain by
Bristol Typesetting Co. Ltd,
Barton Manor, St Philips, Bristol

ISBN 0 234 77764 8

CONTENTS

PREFACE

THE writer on music is sometimes accused of using technical terms as though he did this merely through an inability to express himself in common language. But this 'jargon', as it is sometimes called, contains his terms of reference, and only by its use can he enter into any detailed examination of a composition. His material is entirely subjective, and its expression is formal in the terms of its own particular art. Whereas the literary critic may refer to a character or scene, the music critic is limited to themes, subjects, key relationships and the like. In short, music can be studied only by analysing its form, and the technique that manifests that form.

The first part of this book is therefore devoted to an analysis of Schubert's technique, and if the writer seems to have given him credit for doing what had been done by his predecessors in a similar manner this is only because these methods became part of himself. In that respect they are unique, for they were used to express the thoughts and sentiments of his own individuality. Schubert imbued them with fresh magic, and it is this quality that we should seek for in analysis and rejoice when we have found it. The later chapters deal with the works individually but as many of them have been used to illustrate the earlier chapters there is a fair amount of cross-reference that cannot be avoided.

The compositions can hardly be discussed without reference to their content, but as opinions on the subjective value of a work must necessarily be personal some readers may reject these while others may find them of interest and an incentive to further appreciation of Schubert's piano works.

The chapter on the duets contains some material from the present writer's article 'The pianoforte duets of Schubert' that appeared in the *Musical Times* in November 1928. Thanks are due to J. M. Dent and Son for permission to quote from O. E. Deutsch's *Schubert : a Documentary Biography* and to William Reeves for permission to include the Schumann extract from *Music and Musicians*.

The present writer is also indebted to Dr. Young for his assistance as editor of this book, and to the authors of the books listed in an appendix.

E.G.P.

SCHUBERT'S PIANO WORKS

INTRODUCTION

ALTHOUGH Schubert had such determination of
character that he could reject the steady position of a
schoolmaster and live from hand to mouth in order to
devote his whole time and energy to composition, he had
not the aggressive power necessary to force his way into
the greater world of music. He could not assert himself
among the influential aristocracy, nor adopt an imper-
ious attitude to publishers, as Beethoven did; conse-
quently the demand for his works was sporadic, and the
results, as compared with the performance and publication of that master's works, very unsatisfactory. All who
met Schubert were attracted by him; all who heard his
music admired it: but very few realized his true genius
and his works never received adequate prominent performance or acclamation. His one public concert was
largely a friendly and local affair practically ignored by
the press.

One indication of this lack of encouragement is to be
found in the comparatively large number of incomplete
works, especially for the piano with which we are here
concerned. While it is true that all composers make
sketches and abandon some unfinished works, and that
perhaps Schubertian musicologists have been more
assiduous than others in collecting every scrap of
material of their subject, yet it is a sad fact that with

Schubert there are a number of half or nearly finished works that might have yielded rich results had the incentive been provided by a strong public demand. The absence of any concerto may be partly ascribed to this indifference, for although Schubert was not an executant pianist like Mozart or Beethoven the mind that could produce the C major Symphony and the 'Wanderer' Fantasy could have produced splendid works in this genre for the piano or any other instrument.

However, the rich heritage of Schubert's works which we now possess is not lessened by these imaginary losses, although the fact remains that some fine works were left incomplete for lack of encouragement, while others are incomplete because of lost sections due to the carelessness of their owners, or because publishers produced works piecemeal. It is only now that the ensuing chaos is being brought to order (e.g. the Adagio and Rondo, op.145 and the Sonata in E minor, D 566).

It is difficult to fix an exact figure for the number of piano works. Deutsch lists several which are lost or in a very fragmentary state, and groups some together which are generally considered separately. For example, the *Moments Musicaux* (D780) were published complete in 1828, but two of them had appeared several years earlier. Are the Impromptus two works or eight? The Dances are miscellaneous collections and consist of items composed in various years. The thirty-six in the *Erste Walzer* (op. 9) were written during 1816-21, and the nine waltzes from 1815 were linked with others from 1823-4 and published in 1830 as *Letzte Walzer*. There are about sixty numbers ascribed to the dances in Deutsch but nearly two hundred separate dances were published during Schubert's life and also nearly sixty duets, although the only important solo pianoforte works were the 'Wanderer' Fantasy, two Impromptus (op. 90, nos. 1 and 2), the *Moments Musicaux* and the Sonatas opp. 42, 53 and 78. The reason for the slow appreciation of Schubert's true greatness may be realized by an analysis of the hundred opus numbers published before his death:

56 Songs, either singly or in sets (including song-cycles)
—187 solos

17 Piano duets, some in sets of marches or dances—56 items

8 Dances generally in large sets—193 items

6 Piano solos

9 Choral works; male choruses, church works, and 'Die Advokaten' (which was not really by Schubert! —See D37)

3 Chamber works—opp. 29, 70 and 100

1 Vocal numbers from *Rosamunde*

Thus, excluding the songs, one has to go right back to Bach to find another great composer of such restricted renown with so few major works published during his lifetime, and it is small wonder that he was considered for so long a time as a mere song writer. Schubert never thought of comparing himself with his great predecessors, let alone his powerful contemporary, but he must have realized his own gifts and suffered deeply at times owing to lack of true appreciation and even a modicum of worldly success, and this feeling occasionally found its way into his instrumental works after 1822. His success in the field of song and dance could not compensate for the failure to get his operas, symphonies and other really great works produced, and if we have deplored the unfinished works we must pay tribute to the greatness of mind and unconquerable spirit that could go on composing the symphonies, sonatas, quartets and other masterpieces that now take their place among the greatest.

Although the Schubert catalogue commences with a piano work of 1810 it was another seven years before such works became noticeable. Maurice Brown's careful chronological list (see Bibliography) lists 489 works from 1810 to the end of 1816, and only forty-four are for piano. A numerical list for the whole period will give a clearer idea of the place such works occupy in the total output:

Year	Total works	Pfte. works	Principal works
1810	1	1	Fantasy-duet.
1811	6	1	Fantasy-duet.
1812	21	2	Andante in C, 12 *Deutsche*.
1813	66	11	2 duets, 3 sets dances, solo works short or unfinished.
1814	35	1	Minuet in C sharp minor.
1815	191	12	8 sets of dances, 2 incomplete sonatas.
1816	169	16	11 sets of dances, Allegretto in C, Sonata in E.
1817	90	15	Sonatas—opp. 147 and 164, and in A flat, E minor, D flat and F sharp minor.
1818	34	16	Adagio, 2 incomplete sonatas, 7 duets.

1819	40	6	Sonatas in A (op. 120) and C sharp minor (unfinished).
1820	25	2	Dances.
1821	25	3	Dances, Variation on theme of Diabelli
1822	41	5	Fantasy in C (Wanderer).
1823	35	12	Sonata, op. 143, No. 3 of *Moments Musicaux.*
1824	27	13	Sonata, op. 140 (duet).
1825	42	10	Sonatas, opp. 42, 53 and 'Reliquie'.
1826	41	6	Sonata, op. 78.
1827	41	8	*Impromptus*, opp. 90 and 142. *Moments Musicaux*, nos. 1, 2, 4, 5.
1828	28	7	Sonatas in C, A and B flat. *Drei Klavierstücke.*

This gives a total of piano works (147) related to the full output (958) which is just over one-sixth as compared with the first six years which is one-eleventh, but it must be remembered that a proportion of nearly all forms of composition was unfinished. With reference to the piano works the figures break down into:

	Total works	Completed works
Piano duets	31	31
Piano solos: sonatas	22	13
Piano solos: other large works	4	4

(or 12 if the *Impromptus* and *Klavierstücke* are separated).

	Total works	Completed works
Piano solos: small works	22	14

(or 27, 19 if the *Moments Musicaux* are separated).

| Dances, singly or in sets | 62 | |

Beethoven so dominated the musical world of the nineteenth century that even when Schubert's works became known his piano compositions suffered by an unjust comparison (and it must be noted that his three last sonatas were not published until 1838). It was assumed that because he wrote differently from Beethoven he must be inferior; and because so much stress was placed on form as exemplified by the slightly earlier master any work that did not comply with these theoretical rules must be more or less formless, or at least lacking in 'proper' form. Even as late as 1905 Edmundstoune Duncan could write, 'The simple secret of the inadequacy of Schubert's pianoforte writing in his sonatas, as compared with the full and finished work of Beethoven, is probably explainable by Franz's half-mastery of the instrument.' If this were true it would preclude any composer from producing a great work unless he were a virtuoso on the instrument or instruments for which he wrote.

Although this neglect and misunderstanding of his works may have been partly due to prejudice it was also quite probably due to performance, for the pianist who played a Schubert sonata as he would one by Beethoven must have given a very misleading interpretation. The technique of the two composers, their approach to the instrument, and above all their mentalities were so opposite, and therefore, as appears from contemporary accounts, their methods of touch and tone-production so different, that a true interpretative performance depends on a full realization of these facts. In addition to which an intimate knowledge of Schubert's thought and idioms is, of course, required.

Speaking in general terms Beethoven was much more logical than Schubert for he did not allow side issues to interfere with the development of a work. Schubert on the other hand gave more rein to his fancy and composed in a more uninhibited frame of mind. Being lyrical rather than epic he was not averse to pursuing a sudden inspiration, always with the proviso that this might be adjusted, for although he generally composed at great speed he often inserted alterations or made fair copies with emendations. There are many examples of these alterations in the *Revisionsbericht* which prove that Schubert fully considered the structure of his works and did not let facility of expression run away with purity of thought, so that if he dwelt on certain subjects or episodes and so created a form different from the Beethoven type he did so with a full realization of his procedure.

His method of piano writing may be said to lie midway between that of Beethoven and Chopin. His melodic line is generally wider in range than the former; he was far more chromatic; and he indulged in more ornamentation. Note for example the *Klavierstück* no. 5, the Andante of the unfinished Sonata in C, the B major section of the first of the *Drei Klavierstücke*, the fourth Impromptu of op. 142, and the Adagio (D 612) from which a brief extract is given as Ex. 1 :

Ex. 1.

His range of key was also very wide. The third Impromptu (op. 90) was written in G flat but was altered to G by
the publisher, the fourth opens in E flat minor, as does
the first of the three *Klavierstücke*, while the third
section of the second piece is in A flat minor.[1] The range
of pitch is also extensive—from D_1—f^{111} and indicates
that Schubert had access to the latest pianoforte models.

Although Beethoven's first eight sonatas were written
'for the harpsichord or pianoforte' the latter instrument
had practically ousted the harpsichord by the turn of
the century. Its development had been rapid with
Broadwood, Stodart, Pleyel and Erard, and Stein, who
had invented the shifting keyboard for *una corda*
effects in 1789. His daughter, who was a friend of
Beethoven, and her husband continued improving the
piano so that these Viennese instruments became famous

[1] Note also in later chapters the frequent references to the keys
of G flat and C flat.

for their lightness of touch. Concurrent with this development was the rise of the expert executant. Dussek, Clementi, Czerny, Hummel and John Cramer were some who concentrated on pianoforte technique, and this aspect of performance was developed rather to the detriment of true interpretation and led to mere brilliance or heaviness of tone.

There are many scale and arpeggio passages in Schubert's works that prove his love of brilliance, but a 'thumping' tone he could not abide. He wrote that 'several people assured me that the keys become singing voices under my hands, which, if true, pleases me greatly, since I cannot endure the accursed chopping in which even distinguished pianoforte players indulge'.[1] His brother Ferdinand stated that 'he knew how to treat the instrument with *mastery* and in quite a *peculiar manner*, so that a great specialist in music, to whom he once played his last sonatas, exclaimed "Schubert, I almost admire your playing even more than your compositions!" '[2]

His love for the piano dates from his earliest years. His sister Therese said that he became very friendly with an older relative who was a joiner's apprentice at a pianoforte factory and often went with him to see the work and to play on the instruments. He also practised on an old piano at home, and by the time he was seven and began to take lessons his master found him already very proficient. His father taught him the violin when he was eight and then sent him to the local choir-master for singing lessons. He, Michael Holzer by name, also instructed him in piano and organ playing and in

[1] O. E. Deutsch: *Schubert: A Documentary Biography*, p. 436.
[2] O. E. Deutsch, op. cit., p. 915.

thorough-bass, and it was he who said, 'If ever I wished to teach him anything new I found he had already mastered it',[1] and when he heard him extemporize on a given subject exclaimed, 'He has harmony at his finger-ends!'

This last observation is illuminating, for although Schubert had still much to learn it indicated that he had the gift of counterpoint, for with harmony in his mind he knew exactly where he wanted each note of a chord to progress. The study of harmony teaches where each note of a chord ought to go according to theory; a truly intuitive knowledge may often dictate quite otherwise. Schubert's earliest compositions show that he was completely familiar with all the harmony used by his predecessors, but beyond this he could consider the individual notes of a chord as units in a melodic line. Thus the harmony often became intricate with chromatic passing notes, and the avoidance of chords in their root positions gave the bass a melodic progression which was a true counterpoint to the melody.

Schubert's voice was a valuable asset and when he entered the Chapel Royal Choir and attended the Konvikt[2] at the age of eleven the choral work must have greatly developed his melodic genius so that he could hardly put pen to paper without writing one tuneful phrase after another. Then when his proficiency on the violin and his outstanding musicianship made him the leader of the school orchestra his future was determined and by the age of sixteen he had probably written well over a hundred works of various kinds.

---

[1] Kreissle von Hellborn, *Life of Franz Schubert*, p. 5.
[2] The Imperial Seminary.

The first work of his we have is a piano duet which was written at the age of thirteen and although this was followed by a similar work in the next year it was not until seven years later that he set himself seriously to composition for the pianoforte. He had previously concentrated rather on songs and works that could be performed by vocal and instrumental combinations, although the vast amount of work he did in opera in these early years was unrewarded by performance. His instrumental works showed he had command of sonata form and his many songs and dances proved his mastery of the piano, but yet he seemed reluctant to unite this knowledge in the form of the piano sonata, although he had written three charming sonatinas for piano and violin. Whether it was reluctance or merely the fact that he was engaged so continuously with other forms of composition, and also why he concentrated so much on the sonata form in 1817, are problems difficult to resolve. We do know that in this year he was living with Schober and having given up school-teaching could devote the whole of his time to composition, and very likely he thought this an opportune moment to enter seriously this new field.

Unfortunately there seemed little demand for sonatas and Schubert could get none published until 1826 when one appeared, followed by two in the next year. The Fantasy ('Wanderer') was published in 1823 almost immediately after it was written and it is certainly a point in favour of Cappi and Diabelli that they were so prompt in producing such a big and original work, but they evidently relied rather on the demand for lighter music and accepted dances and duets rather than sonatas

from so melodious a composer. The sonatas that did
appear were by three different publishers. In fact,
Schubert's originality was against him. He could write
neither pseudo-Beethoven nor simple diatonic sonatas in
the style of the early Haydn as did Hummel, Czerny and
others who were mere piano virtuosi with very limited
imaginations that enabled them to concentrate on 'pure
form'. That the publisher Haslinger entitled the G major
Sonata 'Fantasy, Andante, Menuetto and Allegretto'
was an indication that the period of the 'Grand Sonata'
was waning, and Schubert's successors preferred to
express themselves in other forms, for Schumann,
Brahms and Mendelssohn each wrote only three piano
sonatas which were all early works.

Schubert himself probably influenced this revolution,
for he was the first composer to write much piano music
apart from sonatas. His great predecessors wrote
occasional pieces in the form of dances and fantasias, as
did their lesser contemporaries, but it was Schubert who,
by the number of his compositions in the form of
Klavierstücke, Impromptus and *Moments Musicaux*,
brought such music into the foreground. Both Schumann
and Brahms saw the advantages promised by this break-
away and so carried piano composition still further away
from the sonata. More will be said of this in a later
chapter. The main point to note here is that by expressing a wide range of musical thought outside the bounds
of the sonata with lyrical or dramatic interest and with
great harmonic freedom Schubert became the first of
the romanticists and all his successors had to do was to
give additional freedom to these forms.

It is difficult to trace this influence in any detail, for

Schubert had not the wide fame of other composers and much of his piano work remained unpublished for many years. The stature of Beethoven was such, and his works so quickly published, that no one could afford to be ignorant of his works, whereas it was quite possible for many musicians to be comparatively unaware of Schubert's main contributions to music. It is quite common now for writers to remark on resemblances between Schubert and Wagner but it is doubtful whether the latter knew much, if anything, about the former. He would certainly not have made contact through Schumann or Brahms although he may have gained some knowledge through Liszt who was an ardent Schubertian and was influenced in some degree by that fact. Liszt's songs in particular show this—the 'Wanderer's Night Song' with the characteristic Schubert descending bass in thirds and the *Liebestraum* in A flat with its strong resemblance to the Impromptu in G flat in much of the shifting harmonies.

The *Moments Musicaux* may have given more than a hint to Schumann when he composed his many characteristic pieces, especially in the chromatic harmony and the cadences, and the *Nachtstück* in F with its rising sixth and reiterated mediant is surely a tender reminiscence, even if quite unconscious, of one of Schubert's most characteristic finger-prints. But here is not the place to go into any detail on this influence. It would need many pages to supply chapter and verse for such resemblances as would show this and to prove that later composers even knew of the Schubert composition so concerned before they themselves wrote the work in which such influence or resemblance occurred.

II

HARMONY AND MODULATION

As Schubert was in the main stream of music that was flowing very forcefully at the beginning of the nineteenth century it cannot be claimed that he had a direct influence on harmonic development. But he used the classical harmony in his own way to express his individuality and so evolved what may be called the Schubert idiom. His harmonic progressions are always above a firm characteristic bass in which passing notes are often used to form a melodic line, and although his chromatic chords are generally orthodox they are handled in a way particularly his own. They are used quite freely and often with unexpected resolutions, and in this respect he made a valuable contribution to the development of the more free harmonic systems of the following generation.

He was so advanced for his time that even the generally favourable critic of the Leipzig *Allgemeine Musikalische Zeitung* suggested in 1826 that the 'composer now and again hardly knew the ins and outs of the sometimes strange harmonies that visited him (even as regards grammatical writing)'.[1] This was with reference to the Sonata in A minor, op. 42, but in 1824 the critic was very severe about the constant modulations, various progressions and 'strange notation'[2] in a group of songs,

[1]O. E. Deutsch, op. cit., p.513. [2]Ibid. p.354.

mentioning especially the third bar from the end of 'Die Liebe hat gelogen'.

Ex.2.

It is reproduced here as showing that Schubert considered the reader rather than a pedantic harmonic grammar. The seventh on F should resolve to B flat, but as the interval opens out to the octave E it is treated as an augmented sixth, and the last E flat should be altered accordingly to D sharp. Even then the progression is to a six-four chord that does not resolve but passes to a seventh on D and so to C major. Such passages must have been puzzling to the theorists of the time and are still hardly recognized in many of the text-books in frequent use even today.

Not only were Schubert's harmonies very free but discords which had before generally been used as passing chords were used in a much more pronounced manner. Examples of these may be taken from the 1816 Sonata (called *Fünf Klavierstücke*). The trio of the second Scherzo opens with a four-bar sentence in octaves.

Ex.3.

It is basically a passage of descending sixths but what gives it a strong individuality is the emphasis placed on

the accidentals in bar 2 by extending them beyond the
more usual passing reference such as might occur at *b*.
The first Scherzo also opens in octaves with Ex. 4, the
third bar consisting of the notes of a diminished fifth.

Ex.4.

As the movement is in E major some of Schubert's
contemporaries may have considered it a phrase wilfully
distorted by the insertion of the sharp and double-sharp
in bar 3. If on the other hand it is considered as being
in G sharp minor so that this bar is part of a chord on D
sharp we have a movement commencing in the key of
the mediant—and still have to account for the A natural.
Is it an appoggiatura or a suggested Neapolitan sixth?
If so it would resolve on a C sharp minor chord. But the
fifth bar has a chord of E major which is in striking
contrast to any expected harmony, although on repetition of this opening phrase there follows a dominant
seventh on G sharp which resolves to C sharp minor.

As there are no harmonies to this opening four-bar
phrase it may seem academic to discuss the matter but
it is interesting to consider what may have been in
Schubert's mind when the melody occurred to him, and
it illustrates the implications to be found in a simple
phrase of a master. That he has left it enigmatical may
be part of the Scherzo—which means 'joke'—but at bar

26 he presents us with a harmonized and slightly var. version of the phrase in which the diminished interval occurs as part of a dominant seventh on B (Ex. 4b). Other references will be made to this tendency to dwell on discords, but at present the main point to stress is Schubert's facility in introducing various chromatic notes in his melodies without any suggestion of harshness (except when this is necessary) as, for example, in the fifth bar of the opening movement of the above work (a supertonic ninth) and the fifth bar of the Scherzo of the B flat Sonata (a diminished seventh on F sharp in the opening key).

Another point to notice in Schubert's harmonic schemes is the method by which brief modulations appear in phrases in such a manner that the 'foreign' chords seem to belong to the general key of the phrase itself. In the B flat Sonata the first eight-bar sentence is repeated with a slightly altered second half which extends its length to nine bars with a brief incursion of C minor chords that in no way disturbs the even flow of the melody. In the Adagio of the C minor Sonata the repetition of the first four bars after the ninth bar is altered as at Ex. 5 by what appears to be a modulation but which reverts immediately to the original key.

Ex. 5.

In the melodious first subject of the Sonata in A (op. 120) the first bar is harmonized on the tonic and dominant

chords but on its repetition in bar 5 the harmonies are
a diminished seventh on A sharp leading to a B minor
chord and so back to E and A major. Then follows a
short reference to C sharp major that closes very gracefully in A again. This change is a characteristic Schubertian touch. It is true that there are chords of F sharp
minor in this short passage and that this is the relative
minor of the original key, but the dominant of this
minor key is so much in evidence that the aural result is
one of brightness from the prevalence of A and C sharp
major. And such passages flow so serenely that one feels
that Schubert is using harmonies from adjacent or even
remote keys as what may be called colour effects. He
harmonizes any note or phrase with any major or minor
chord that will intensify its significance whenever he
feels this to be necessary.

The Adagio of the *Fünf Klavierstücke* is in C major
but the key of D minor is suggested by the fifth bar and
leads to Ex. 6a at bars seven and eight, but then carries

Ex: 6.

on further in C. The opening is then repeated until bar 7 which is altered to Ex. 6b as though for further modulation, but the harmonies of the falling semiquavers are a mixture of F and D minor that descend gracefully to the six-four chord on G and so to the full close.

In the sixth of the *Moments Musicaux* there is an instance somewhat similar to this and to Ex. 3, where the E sharp is a mere passing note between the E of the first chords and the F sharp of the fourth.

Ex. 7.

But the note is not only dwelt upon for a whole bar but accentuated by the top C sharp as though the chord were the third inversion of a seventh on that note, in which case the bass should fall to A sharp. That we do not sense this failure to resolve in the usual manner is due to the skill of the part-writing and because the note B is used as a pedal note. In fact the passage is an elaboration of a dominant six-four chord resolving to a five-three in bar 4 by way of the passing notes in bar 3. It will be noted also that even in bar 4 the resolution of the original six-four chord is deferred to the end of the bar by the movement of the upper parts.

Such harmony is characteristic of Schubert, and although he modulated very frequently and often startlingly it is a fact that quite often no change of key really takes place. This is also another explanation of the

B

'strange notation' complained of by the critic, for
Schubert regarded many notes and chords outside the
range of his key as consisting of passing notes and inserted the accidentals as part of his counterpoint instead of
as pure harmonic progressions. A very simple example of
this occurs in the opening of the 'Wanderer' Fantasy at
the third and sixth bars, first with a C sharp above the
dominant chord in C so that the upper part moves in
semitones—B, C, C sharp, D; and then with a D sharp
between D and E to give the upper part another semitone rise from C sharp to E—passages which also upset
the Leipzig critic in 1823, especially as these phrases
are inverted in the reprise at bars 72 and 75 so that the
rising semitones are in the bass, with the C sharp below
a dominant chord and the D sharp below a tonic chord,
still in the key of C major.

In the opening of the A minor Sonata, op. 42 there are
also some sharp dissonances formed by the moving parts
in a series of chords.

Ex. 8

The third bar passes from tonic to dominant with a descending bass that forms an augmented sixth on F natural (Ex. 8a) in which the E of the tenor is still maintained as an inner 'pedal'. This is answered two bars later, not by a smooth phrase such as 8b but by the wide open chord of 8c which emphasizes the dissonance of the E above the F sharp and their fall to F natural and D sharp of the augmented sixth. In the reprise 8a is inverted and the fifth chord is altered to a diminished fifth, and its answer toned down considerably to the form of 8b.

Such progressions abound in Schubert's works, but that he could write beautifully in plain diatonic harmony is evident on many a page of his music, although it was natural for him to elaborate the harmonies in the more emotional sections in a distinctive manner. The Allegretto of the Sonata in G, op. 78, proceeds for thirty-six bars almost wholly in tonic and dominant harmony, and even after that the sharps on A and C serve merely as passing notes until a slightly mounting excitement leads to a repetition of the opening subject; making fifty-five bars without a modulation or even the suggestion of one.

The Allegretto of the second of the *Drei Klavierstücke* is also very simple in harmonic outline. It commences in E flat and modulates to the dominant at bar 9. The next sentence reverts to E flat and although its second phrase goes into the tonic minor it closes in the dominant and so back to the final sentence in the home key. One interesting point is that at bars 19 and 23 a lower appoggiatura is dwelt upon which is similar to one in the sonata mentioned above and to one that occurs in the sixth of the *Moments Musicaux* at the seventh bar where a chord of the dominant seventh is retarded for a whole bar over the tonic chord. This short work is full of such impressive retardations, many whole bars consisting of various kinds of sevenths resolved in devious ways, but generally by the bass or treble descending a semitone. Apart from the beauty of the work it should be a mine of information for the harmony student.

Such harmonies served the emotion of Schubert's melodies and were indeed born with them and very rarely did he alter them in his sketches. They often appear quite unexpectedly and resolve unpredictably and at times surge in great waves without key stability at a climax. This is to be found especially in the songs where all could be justified by the trend of the verse, but Schubert did not write in this rhetorical manner in his instrumental works unless it appeared justified, as in the *Moment Musical* just mentioned, for the detailed work to be found in the songs would generally be out of proportion in the bigger compositions.

For example, the eighteen bars of rushing discords which make the fifth stanza of 'An Schwager Kronos' so vivid would generally be much too concentrated in a piano work, and we find that a somewhat similar passage in the 'Wanderer' Fantasy at the climax of the third movement which leads into the final Allegro consists of forty-six bars. The harmonic outline is given in Ex. 9, and each of the first twelve chords occupies a whole bar.

Ex.9.

Then the upper parts swing into big arpeggios and most chords cover two, four or eight bars as indicated by the figures above. There are several similar passages throughout the work, although not so long, and this one is especially notable for the lengthy duration of the augmented sixth (Ex. 9B), and its contrast with the diminished seventh on A natural which is the first chord to be sustained through several bars (Ex. 9A).

Augmented Sixth

This procedure is reversed in the third Impromptu of op. 90.[1] At bar 72 the augmented sixth on A flat follows the chords of C, F minor, and C, but this phrase is repeated immediately with the harmonies of C, F major, and C, and the following chord is a diminished seventh

[1] The references here are to the transposed edition in G.

on A natural resolving likewise on the dominant of the
home key. Twenty-one bars from the end this chord is
on E flat following the chord of C minor, but eight bars
later it follows one of A flat minor in its first inversion.
The passionate outburst in the Impromptu, op. 142, no.
2, is resolved with this sixth. The placid opening in A flat
passes to D flat and then crashes into the chord of G flat
minor which is changed to an augmented sixth that runs
through its three forms as the melody falls with a 5–4–
3 movement. This has an unexpected resolution, if it can
be so called, which turns into another 5–4–3 fall and so
back to the opening melody. If Schubert had been writing
merely pretty music he would at least have passed from
the first sixth to the second, bringing the melody down
from the top F flat through the flats of E, D, C, B, and A
and so to E flat for the usual resolution to A flat; but that
ffz interjection of the third bar in Ex. 10 has a wonderful
dramatic effect.

Ex.10.

Such harmonic variations are an essential part of
Schubert's thought, and an interposed chord, a delayed
resolution, or even a normal one with the parts placed
unexpectedly—as in the above example or in the leap to
the high A in Ex. 8c—always provide a pleasant surprise.
Another example may be taken from the Impromptu,

op. 90, no. 3, where the Neapolitan sixth in bar 61 is in
an E minor phrase but the melody drops from C to E
and resolves in the key of C major.

Ex.11.

In bars 92-3 the melody is the same but the chord below
E is the dominant B and the usual resolution takes place
except that it leads to the tonic major key.

Neapolitan Sixth

This is one of Schubert's favourite chords not only
for its truly pathetic effect, as in the cadence to the first
sentence of the episode in the Allegretto of the G major
Sonata, but as a passing chord such as is found in the B
minor section of the second Impromptu (op. 90) where
it is used in bar 18 to interrupt the F sharp minor
cadence, and in bar 62 for a similar purpose but different
key, and in bar 44 as a fierce interjection. In its root
position this major chord on the flattened supertonic
often occupies a dual position, being either a chromatic
or common triad according to its relationship with what
follows or has preceded it, as is found in the changes
between the tonalities of E and F, and B flat and A in the
D major Sonata (op. 53). Even when not actually present
its effect is generally sensed when there is a semitone
shift of key, and as Schubert often modulated up or
down by this degree it has given rise to the phrase

eapolitan key' in reference to his works. It may be
observed in the last of the *Drei Klavierstücke* at the
change from C to D flat and in Scherzo I (D593),
where the second part in D flat modulates to C minor in
preparation for the return to the home key of B flat.
There is also the change from the chord of D flat to F, in
which the bass note is C (bar 24), in the modulatory
episode of op. 164, and the progress from G flat to F
major (bar 50) at the end of the second subject; and
although the first is covered by the rather unexpected
appearance of the six-three chord above the bass C, and
the second by the interposition of two other chords, there
is clearly the Neapolitan relationship.

Schubert's contemporaries considered that he modulated too freely, but it has been shown that many passages
are harmonic effects within the key and not real modulations. He used major chords on various degrees of the
scale much more than had been done before, and as in
many cases these were not immediately resolved within
the key it appears as though the key had been deserted
for the time being. But these passages do close in the
home key and therefore negate the true purpose of a
modulation from one key to another. One such case has
already been noted. This is in bars 10-12 in the Sonata,
op. 120, where the harmonies could have been on the
mediant and submediant but the first is made a major
triad of the mediant, in spite of which the sentence
closes on the home tonic of A.

Diminished Seventh

A simple example of a somewhat similar nature occurs
in the Presto of the 'Wanderer' Fantasy. This movement

opens in A flat and works its way to C flat. On this key-
note there is an extended diminished seventh (bars 75-
78) which normally should resolve into some other key.
It was a much over-worked chord, but probably never
before used in this manner for it 'resolves' in the preced-
ing key of C flat. Schubert used this effect some years
later in 'Die Stadt' where the diminished seventh which
pervades the song over a bass C is 'resolved' in the same
way by a final C and has caused much discussion; but
if these two cases are related we must conclude that
Schubert considered this progression a natural one that
justified itself.

Modulatory episode

The general purpose of the modulatory passage was
to lead from one section or subject to another in a different key by a gradual process in what may be described
vaguely as panoramic form. It avoided a harsh juxtaposi-
tion of keys and led the listener from one subject to
another in an easy and logical manner. This 'rule' was
occasionally broken for the sake of excitement or surprise
such as is often found in Haydn's works, but Beethoven
developed both methods, sometimes using a transition
in which reminiscences of the first subject or premoni-
tions of the following one occurred and in other places
making a sudden and electrifying change of key direction. Schubert also used both these methods and invented
a third which may be termed the pleasant short cut.
Although he was not the first to use it he may be credited
with bringing it to perfection, for he used it even in his
two greatest symphonies.

The most famous example is the bridge passage of the

Unfinished Symphony in which the two horns sound
the dominant and then open out to the tonic chord
(Ex. 12a), but it has an exact parallel in the pianoforte
Allegretto (D.915) which links the opening C minor
subject with its major version (Ex. 12c).

Ex. 12.

As written above they are quite commonplace fragments
of music, but the first is elevated to great expressiveness
by its orchestration and context, and the second by its
chording and context. The minor subject has descended
in fortissimo phrases to the dominant after which there
is a bar rest. Then follows the transition to the major,
not in the plain outline of Ex. 12b, but in the close
harmony of Ex. 12c. This simple formula for modulation
which Lavignac calls childish and hackneyed is quite
charming as used by Schubert. It occurs quite openly
in the form of Ex. 12b in the Rondo of the D major

Sonata at bar 18 and serves to bring the second sentence, which is in A back to the opening key of D, and is used in each repetition of the first subject. It also appears in the C minor Sonata. The modulatory episode works its way to a close on the chord of B flat and the second subject opens in E flat with the rising bass of dominant to tonic and the falling treble, this time from submediant to tonic.

In the B flat Sonata the first subject closes on the dominant seventh. This is changed to a diminished seventh which becomes enharmonically the dominant ninth of F sharp minor when the bass falls to C sharp and the new subject appears. It is outlined in Ex. 13a, and if this is compared with bars 18-19 it will be noted that there an even shorter modulation takes place as the subject closes in the tonic and then reappears in G flat— which is F sharp major—merely by the introduction of a C flat in the bass which descends to the tonic of the new key (Ex. 13b).

Ex.13.

In the reprise *a* is repeated but by a slight alteration of the three last chords the second subject appears in the key of B minor. Here we have a transition consisting of four bars only, and although that in the A minor Sonata, op. 143 occupies fourteen bars it consists of a mere couple of preliminary harmonic suggestions. The first subject closes on bare octaves for both hands on the falling phrase of C to A. These two notes are echoed very softly four times a tone lower on B flat and G, and then with a forte clash a semitone higher on B natural and G sharp which expand, still merely in double octaves, to the notes of the chord of E major in which key the second subject duly enters fifteen bars from the previous close in A minor. The brevity of the passage consists in its economy of harmony which is really only the inter-position of the B flat and G, and the expansion of the passage is for building up a huge climax that serves as a background for the ensuing pianissimo subject.

Most of the transitions in the smaller piano works are very brief, and some rather pedestrian as though Schubert merely turned the corner to a fresh aspect, probably because he did not wish to detract from the subjects as might be done by a vivid modulatory passage. In op. 90, no. 4 the transition from first to second subject is made by turning the closing chord of A flat major into a seventh and using it as a dominant seventh to C sharp minor, in which key the new subject immediately commences, but as this is largely chromatic a modulatory passage of any length would detract from the contrast of the new subject with the previous diatonic passages.

The opening twenty-four bars of op. 90, no. 2 are in E flat major but bar 25 commences immediately in the tonic minor and the rapid triplets really cover a sequence of sevenths outlined in Ex. 14, and continued modulation leads to the return of the opening subject.

Ex. 14.

This middle section is development and the contrasting section occurs later in B minor which is introduced by bringing the first subject to E flat minor, changing it suddenly to G flat major and using this chord enharmonically as the dominant of B minor. This new subject, like the first, modulates freely so that a long transition passage would have detracted from the brilliance of both.

The weakest transitions are to be found in the *Drei Klavierstücke*. Brief modulatory passages such as those quoted above are quite suitable for linking various episodes, especially when they continue the figuration of the previous subject, but having used such a device in the Impromptu Schubert should not have repeated the process in the first of these *Klavierstücke*. It suggests a touch of laziness or, to say the least, a lack of that interest which he so constantly applied to details that eluded his sheer inspiration. In the second number the second subject closes with plain reiterated chords which gradually change from C to E flat, a modulation interesting in itself but, if one may use the phrase, rather flat-footed; later it modulates from A flat minor to E flat by means of prolonged chords. There are similar methods of transition in the third number and it is to be hoped that Schubert would have revised these brief sections if time had permitted (see p. 127).

The transition passages in the sonatas are all interesting and two have already been mentioned. In the Sonata in A major (1828) the first movement recapitulation is prepared, after the development has reached a chord of E. by fourteen bars continuing in that key and then introducing its seventh and so leading to the home key by the last bar which unobtrusively makes use of an inversion of Ex. 12b as the treble rises chromatically from E to A, and the bass falls from G sharp by semitones to A. On the other hand the second subject, at bar 55, enters after a splendid example of what Tovey calls the 'enhanced' dominant, for at bar 39 there is a full close in B major in which key the first subject still continues for several bars and the passage seems to settle down more firmly until a brief passing A natural brings in the second subject in E, and in spite of all the previous A sharps this seems inevitably the right key.

In the 'Reliquie' the first subject closes in C and here and in the ensuing two bars in B flat the bass takes up the rhythm of Ex. 15 for one bar, and this figure enters more frequently until it is alone for four bars in G, and four bars later it appears in B minor as the bass of the second subject. The harmonic scheme of this transition

Ex.15.

is very interesting as the B flat bars just mentioned pass to A flat which then proceeds as in Ex. 15, through B minor and back again to A flat and then to G and B minor. This process is repeated in the reprise but the final chord is changed to minor, which is repeated with F flat in the bass. An enharmonic change brings us to

E major as in Ex. 15b, the last bar having a striking effect owing to the sudden introduction of an augmented sixth at *x* on the flat supertonic followed by the dominant chord.

Although the modulations are interesting in themselves it is the key relationships involved that are even more characteristic of Schubert's style. He often went far afield even for the key of the second subjects in his sonatas. Changes to adjacent keys are common, sometimes for the surprise so caused, but at other times by a gradual but brief transition as at bar 46 of op. 15 ('The Wanderer'). There has been a modulation to G and the treble, as a solo, takes up the third of the chord, plays on it with a kind of slow turn and then descends to G sharp as the third of an E major chord. There are many such changes in the Sonata in D, the first subject swinging between D and F; the exposition ending in A to change immediately after the double bar to B flat; and the second subject commencing in G after a close in A. The Menuetto of the 'Reliquie' commences in A flat and proceeds to A in this manner (Ex. 16), the phrase *a* being repeated twice and then continuing as shown. This

Ex. 16.

section concludes in the same manner but with delusive effect, for as it is a semitone higher we expect to arrive in the key of B flat, but the key signature is changed to A flat and the music itself proceeds to G flat as the subdominant of D flat !

The three-two section of the third of the *Drei Klavier-stücke* is in D flat after a passage in C, and later returns to that key. Scherzo II is in D flat but at bars 14-15 there is a rising scale passage in octaves that ends on E flat which is treated as a leading note to the key of E, with a change of signature from five flats to four sharps thus modulating up by an augmented second. It is impossible to quote more than these few examples but the conclusion to be drawn from them all is that harmony was used much more for its colourful and emotional effect, as well as an adjunct to form, by Schubert than by previous composers, and this effect was most often dependent on the use of the major third. His partiality for minor sevenths was due to the fact that the discord resolved on to a third, and diminished sevenths were often expanded to minor sevenths to achieve this effect. A long turn on the leading note frequently occurs as it involves the major third of the dominant, and it is particularly noticeable in the last A major sonata. Previous mention has been made of the use of secondary major triads. And Schubert was not always satisfied with the mere triad but often gave its mediant prominence either in treble or bass. The second subject of op. 143 has a more striking character in the reprise because the third becomes the upper note instead of the previous tonic, and the opening phrase of op. 78 generally appears with the major third in the melody while its place is taken by the minor third in the more agitated development. When the 'Wanderer' Fantasy modulates to G it is followed by the key of E with the third above; and the magical effect of the Adagio theme, when it arrives in the tonic major, is due chiefly to the E sharp in the melody as the third of the chord in the second bar. In the last movement of op. 143 the A minor subject bursts suddenly into a big arpeggio of B flat but this is not a modulation for it is followed immediately by a return to A minor. Its significance lies in the tonal contrast for bar 23 consists of a series of minor thirds so that the following B flat major chord comes like a flash of light.

A beautiful example of the use of the major third is to be found in the slow movement of op. 53. The first complete bars pass from dominant to mediant and then back again, but the brightness is clouded by the harmony (Ex. 26a, p. 55), and it is not until twelve bars later after the *rit.* that the mediant realizes its true purpose (Ex. 26b), enhanced by the previous phrase in C, and passes happily to the tonic instead of, as previously, rather sadly to the dominant. This cadential phrase occurs several times in its original key and more times in passing harmonies and is an important factor in making this the happiest of all Schubert's slow movements. Indeed, all through the sonata the major mediant appears prominently time after time—in the arpeggios of the first movement, the middle section of the Scherzo and in the Trio. In the Rondo it takes its place immediately in the accompaniment and in the slower section.

III

MELODY, RHYTHM AND FORM

T H E S E subjects are so interrelated that it is somewhat difficult to treat them separately. The form of a work, apart from its classification such as 'first movement' or 'rondo', depends on the continuity of its thought, the relationship of its parts and its inner logical processes. These are what constitute its holding power over the listener, and they in turn depend on the melody and harmony in which rhythm is embodied. The overall rhythmic impulse of a composition may be broken down into small sections and indeed we refer to various bar-lengths of rhythm, but these would be disjunct without some bigger embracing rhythm or form that is like a developing life-force giving the work unity and finality.

It seems that music must generally consist of short phrases and sentences for this is how thought functions. The mind may envisage a very big idea in words or sound but the process of expressing it necessitates a step by step progress in which one statement follows another in logical order, and it is when this sequence is not main-tained that formlessness or unintelligibility results. The composer, however, does share with the writer—as distinct from other artists—the advantage of presenting his work in time, and this allows him to break one thread of his discourse in order to develop others and then bring them together by some assertion of their relationship which satisfies the suspense caused by the break.

The musical movement in time is theoretically infinite and progresses in regular beats according to its time signature. It is the notes within the bar that put curvature and a period to this straight line, and the value of these undulations as a mode of expression depends on the composer's inspiration. But the single bar is seldom self-sufficient. It may serve for a figure or theme but it takes several bars to constitute a rhythm just as a good many words are necessary to establish a poetic rhythm. There is another similarity here, for as it is not so much the mere words as their selection and arrangement that constitutes fine poetry, so it is the choice succession of notes in a melody that ensures a vital rhythm. An uninspired tune merely marks time, but a good one progresses. It carries the mind forward, but for only a brief period, and it is on the ensuing phrases and their capacity to continue this process that the form of a work will be judged. Not even the ability to write fine sentences makes a great writer or composer for it is the power to create an evolutionary process of exposition that grows to some definite climax or conclusion that is the hall-mark of a masterpiece.

Descending to details we may first note the form of the Schubertian phrase and sentence. No. 5 of *Moments Musicaux* consists metrically of a crotchet and two quavers to the bar, but its rhythm depends chiefly on harmony and accentuation. The first four-bar phrase is answered by a repetition in which there is merely a change of chord positions. This might form an eight-bar sentence except for the fact that there is no final cadence;

and it is followed by a modulatory passage with a continued rise in pitch and accent to the extent of thirteen
bars. Hence from the regular and inconclusive pulsation
of the first part the ear and mind are carried forward
by the succeeding rise in pitch and volume to a climax
of four fortissimo chords on D flat (in the key of F
minor) and a further rise before a close on the dominant.
The first number of this set likewise commences with
two four-bar phrases but with quite a different rhythm.

Ex.17.

In the first phrase bar 3 imitates the first bar and bar 4
elaborates the second. Then follows a tonic minor version of bar 4 which breaks out in a new direction and
passes through several tonalities to a full close, forming
a four-bar response to the opening quoted above.

Many of Schubert's movements open in similarly
trenchant style, but he also had a more deliberate style
depending on the use of the anacrusis. The sixth of the

Moments Musicaux gives an example of the up-beat followed by a long chord with a suspension. The second number elaborates the up-beat to form a short and delayed movement of the phrase for a whole bar, as in the delightful Trio to the popular *Marche Militaire* (D51 no. 1) which commences with four reiterated notes. This 'springboard' effect commences the second subject of the second of the *Moments Musicaux* (Ex.43a, p. 112) both subjects of op. 90, no. 1 (Ex. 20), and, with slight variation, the opening of the Sonata in G. This reiterated figure of three or four notes or chords became of great import to Schubert and was often used most effectively. It occurs in the fifth *Moment Musical* as a fierce interjection, in the B minor section of op. 90, no. 2, in the finale of the C minor Sonata in modified form, and in the finale of the last symphony with effective and tremendous force. It may be used as a moment of deliberation or of gathering energy, and may even be the origin of such prolonged 'call' notes as introduce the first and last of the Impromptus.

Dance music must of course be quite regular in form and various devices must be used to avoid monotony. When the waltz got quicker it became possible to treat the bass as a six-four or even twelve-four tempo and use it to support a broad melody, but the Ländler and Waltz of Schubert's day had not enough speed or length for this and hence a more lively melody was necessary and he varied his phrasing in many ways. They are generally in eight- or sixteen-bar sections. The first of the twelve *Deutsche Tänze* (D 420) has one of each, but the first (of sixteen bars) is in two similar halves except for the concluding cadences. These have to consist for dance

purposes of two equal sections and although the basic
rhythm is regular the melodic one is not. Here it is (Ex.
18a):

There is a sort of compression in the middle which ex-
pands as the melody reaches its peak in bar 5 which is
repeated, and is marked *fp.* rather to stress the halfway
line than for mere expression. A second-rate composer
would have dotted the first D, made it fall to A in the
next bar and then commenced the next phrase so that it
rose on A, D, F sharp in the fifth bar and so cut out that
little repetition. In fact, Schubert carries out this form
in his next section as though to emphasize the infor-
mality of the first part. (Ex. 18b). Note the final com-
bination of the beginning and the end of the previous
example.

A glance at the sixth of this set will show a further
departure from the norm for bars 6 and 7 imitate in
sequence the two previous bars, and thus the fourth bar
seems melodically to belong to the second phrase, and
the eighth bar repeats the previous one. The harmony

changes in bar 5 to supply a metrical balance but the melody is $3+2+2+1$. The ensuing section is quite regular in delightful two-bar sequences. The whole of the dances are well worth examination for their phrasing alone, and as very many of them might be considered technically as studies over a tonic and dominant bass they are worthy of setting beside Beethoven's Diabelli Variations, the one set as an expression of sheer lightheartedness and the other of mental concentration.

In the bigger works there is of course room for much broader effects and the necessity in the more lyrical movements for much longer cantabile passages. The theme of the variations in op. 42 is itself deceptive. As written it consists of two sixteen-bar sections with the second only repeated, but the first is really an eight-bar sentence repeated with variations and this sentence itself consists of two halves which are almost the same except for the cadence. The second half of the theme begins with a four-bar phrase which is repeated but with an altered cadence, and the last eight bars consist of the opening four bars plus a variation of the same. Hence the theme itself is a miniature set of variations on the phrases found in bars 1-4 and 17-20 so that the basic form is

$$a+a+(a+a)+b+b+a+a$$

although none of the a's or b's are exactly alike and it is the subtle harmonic touches and chord positioning that avoids all sense of monotony. In the variations proper the section marked in brackets is omitted (except for the last) so that they consist of $8+16$ bars, with each section repeated.

The Andante of op. 120 commences on the first beat the bar, but surely the second phrase begins as marke below Ex. 19 in spite of Schubert's phrase marks?

Ex.19.

At any rate this is clear in bars 9 and 10 where the melody rises up to prepare for the appoggiatura; it is this appoggiatura that permeates the whole movement and the presence or absence of its anacrusis that gives such charm to it. The alteration of the phrasing after the first bar is what justifies the cadence in bar 7, for the eighth bar begins the next sentence with a quotation of the opening bar, and the addition of an extra phrase in bar 13 produces a complete eight-bar sentence.

The Impromptus op. 90 provide several illustrations of phrase extension. The contours of the four-bar phrases on the first page of no. 1 provide plenty of variety, but in the flowing melody of the following subject a further placidity is obtained by a five-bar rhythm. This is accomplished by extending what would normally be one bar to two, which are sustained not only by the triplet accompaniment but by the suggestion of counter-melody in the tenor (Ex.20).

This is repeated with a beautiful modulation from A flat to C flat, but in the following phrase, which leads back to the original key, the equivalent of the minim

Ex. 20.

section is in crotchets thus turning the phrase into one of four bars.

In the next Impromptu the running triplets conceal a series of three- and four-bar phrases as the first descending passage really concludes in the third bar, but as it is on a first inversion we are led to the ascending passage of bar 4 and so to a four-bar phrase which answers the first. The form is thus really 3 + 2 overlapping to form 4, answered by 4: or 3 + 1 + 4. This is repeated twice with modifications and leads to the modulatory passage quoted on p. 31. (Ex. 14). All this gives the listener a general impression of four-bar phrases but what he really hears is three eight-bar sentences with internal convolutions that keep the ear alert.

The simple melody of no. 3 is also delightful in form despite its continued four-bar rhythm. Any sense of formality is avoided by the use of crotchets in bar 6. If they had been minims the seventh bar would have formed a full close a bar later, but as it is on a first inversion it carries forward to a close in the dominant, and so to a repetition of the subject that does lead to a full close. This melodic form allows for lingering cadences which add to the placidity of the opening pages and brings into relief the emotional excitement that follows later.

In the trio section of the last of these Impromptus the first eight bars are followed by a sentence of seven bars with an additional modulating bar. This sentence has an effect of striving to rise for four bars but only reaches E as an appoggiatura to D sharp; but when it appears again near the end of the trio the four bars are extended to eight and gradually rise to G sharp. In the F sharp minor section of the second *Moment Musical* we get what might be called a pre-view of the subject in the first few bars, simple in harmony and short in length. It is a six-bar phrase and is followed by a repetition in full length of eight bars with the harmonies altered. It is repeated again later, without the introductory phrase, and the last half of it modulates into the tonic major with beautiful effect.

These are but a few examples to show how Schubert's skill in rhythm could instil a magic quality into simple phrases. We have ample proof that he could produce the most wonderful melodies, but we also generally find on examination that they come from very simple elements. If Ex. 20 had been written all in crotchets as a four-bar phrase it would have been a commonplace tune, but as it stands it has all the grace of a poetic verse with a lingering middle phrase (as for example 'Now fades the glimmering landscape on the sight'). The commencement of op. 90, no. 3 can hardly be described as having a notable melody but its form, as noted previously, and the gradual changing harmonies clothe it with serenity. It is in such passages as these that the basic charm of the composer lies. Like the poet Wordsworth who opens our eyes to the inner beauty of the commonplace so does Schubert by the frequent use of common musical phrases enable us to perceive their capacity for deep musical expression, and, as we know by experience, this expressiveness is developed throughout the composition.

But there are other aspects of Schubert's work to be considered for he was also passionate, dramatic and at times tragic. Such expressions generally demand great freedom of rhythm and form, for they often entail the development of phrases and thematic fragments. The Sonata op. 42 opens with two simple two-bar phrases (Ex. 8, p. 21) the first melodic and without harmony, the second fully harmonized. They are quite distinct and yet have an indescribable relationship in spite of their points of opposition. The first has a wide range of pitch and insists on the notes of the tonic chord; the second is static in its more obvious upper parts except for the final rise and concentrates rather on the dominant triad with its major third, for the cadential fall is to that note and an inner melody in the right hand part descends by step from E to G sharp. This cadence does not lead back to the tonic but to a repetition of the first phrase a tone higher, as though suggesting its pliability, and is answered by a broader version of *a* (see Ex. 8c). Hence there is an opposition between minor and major thirds and the movement develops this conflict as though it sought not only to smooth out the sharp contours of the first phrase but confirm the ascendancy of the major triad. That this contest is not merely technical but one between moods as well as modes must be left to the listener to decide. Such mental states as are here expressed in music cannot be noted definitely in words for each person can only interpret them from his own knowledge and experience, but we can analyse the form which this conflict assumes, noting the metamorphosis of the themes, and their varying rhythmic patterns, as they wax and wane throughout the movement.

A   Bars   1—10   The main subject with its two contrasting motifs *a* and *b*.

B   11—25   A 'modulating' passage in which each section asserts a major influence at its climax in E, F, and B flat.

C   26—39   a development of *b*: although with a very decided rhythm the chords are reversed so that those in the minor occur on the strong beats. But bar 29 modulates to C major so that the major thirds become prominent. Further chromatic chords lead to

D   40—61   Second subject in C, its rhythm being derived from bar 12. This cannot maintain its key but goes to D minor at bar 44, returning in bar 52 with the rhythm of *b* and repeating it in D minor, and closing on dominant discords and long significant rests.

E   63—90   commencing with *a* and versions of *b* in C minor, modulating to C major with similar treatment but *a* now appears in a version with more conjunct movement and extended to two bars.

90—165 Development devoted wholly to *a*. It works up to a big climax and then *a* passes through various keys in canon commencing ppp.

166—185 Section B enlarged and varied to lead to A minor.

186—199 Section C exactly repeated but for the last two bars which are altered to lead to A major.

200—222 Section D repeated in A major and B minor: a third lower.

223—231 Return of first subject in A minor but *a* closes each time on 6/4 – 5/3 chord on the dominant and so loses its major emphasis. It does not expand as it did at first. See Ex. 8 *b* and 8 *c*.

232 to end A magnificent coda commencing with the first subject and continuing on the lines of E and the first part of the development section, but at bar 263 there is a big crescendo descent to F major and then a version of *b* enters *ff*. At bar 271 *a* enters for the last time in its original form. It is followed by a repetition of the previous passage although the descending phrase ends on F sharp instead of F, but strong modulation and ever rising phrases still lead to the home key and the movement concludes with a most determined statement of a further transformed version of *b*, so that it commences and ends very firmly on the tonic and makes but brief reference to its minor third.

Much more could be added with regard to the rhythmic phrasing of the progressive appearances of the various themes and the build up of the climaxes. It might be noted that although Schubert is often accused of making too much of his second subject we have in this sonata a mere twenty-one bars, which would be insignificant except for the fact that this is the only section that is conclusively in the relative, and later, the tonic major of the key. Also, after the big climax in the middle of the work the first theme steals into its original key at bar 151 and so appears to be the reprise but for its further development and the absence of its answering phrase. In the reprise the second phrase of the first subject is modified from Ex. 8c to 8b.

Compared with this movement which has a complicated form-rhythm of fragmentary 'motives', nearly all closely related, that of the other Sonata in A minor (op. 143) is quite simple in general outline:

	First Subject	Modulation	Second Subject	Coda	Development
	46	14	14	29	62 bars
Reprise	47	6	14	59	

The first subject however is in two parts of 8+13 connected by a four-bar link which is very similar to the modulating section; and these two parts are repeated with slight but significant alterations without the link. The shortness of the second modulatory transition is due to its exciting section being abstracted and used in the final coda where it prepares for the concluding cadences, and the extra bar in the first subject enables the phrase to ascend higher than at first.

The scherzos are necessarily full of rhythmic variety and their quick tempo is an important factor in this. The opening of the Scherzo in op. 42 if played slowly and with no accent on the minim would sound like a four-bar phrase with an extended cadence, but at 'allegro vivace', with the syncopated fortissimo chord, it becomes one of five bars.

Ex. 21.

It is followed, piano, by five bars but similar treatment urges the rhythm forward through another three bars and as this ends on an inversion of a dominant ninth on G we are carried still further to the full close in C at bar 22—the cadence in bar 15 being so short as to be passed over almost without notice. The rhythm of the initial figure of two quavers and a minim in Ex. 21 forms the basis of most of the movement. Sometimes it forms short sets of sequences in various keys, at others it introduces four-bar phrases, and also forms an accompaniment as two quavers and a crotchet, and in one way and another occurs seventy times throughout the movement.

The Scherzo of the Sonata in D has a tremendous drive owing to its speed and cross accents. The opening rhythm is in alternate two and four beats against the three-four time for eight bars. The following contrasting section swings along in six beats with the accent on an off-beat. Exx. 22a and 22b give the rhythm of each.

Ex.22.

In the later B flat section the treble continues the *a* rhythm, and in the bass, which has even crotchet beats, the middle one in each bar is accented for the first four bars in the first part and for six bars in the repeat so that the rhythm is smoothed out into the normal three-four.

The Scherzo of the last Sonata has a delicate, tripping movement, partly due to the constantly recurring rhythm of crotchets and quavers (Ex. 23) with which it commences, and partly to the little figure of Ex. 23b that is also frequent.

Ex.23.

The trio has a fascinating cross-rhythm: the treble being like the Scherzo of Ex. 22a, but with crotchets instead

C

of the dotted rhythm—thus hardly recognizable as similar, especially as it is in B flat minor, and the bass with alternating rests of one and three beats. (Ex. 24).

Ex. 24.

The overlapping of phrases is a common method of attaining continuity but one cannot refrain from quoting the beautiful dolce section in the finale of op. 122 (after the double bar). Here the phrases are one and a half bars long, with connecting runs in the intervening half-bars; so they may be considered as two-bar phrases commencing with the first beat or, after the first bar and a half, commencing in alternate half-bars. Thus it proceeds with the melody in the right hand to a full close in bar 10, where the left hand (in the tenor) immediately takes up the melody on the first beat and continues for only nine bars. At this point the treble takes over again, and then the tenor, so that there are four sentences of $10+9+10+9 = 35$ bars. There is a full close at the end of each sentence and these are all alike except in key; but their finality is destroyed by the overlap of the final and initial phrases of each sentence, so that the listener is carried right along to bar 35 without a break. To this must be added the fact that the melody is really all in two-bar phrases, none of them being exactly alike because of variation in contour or key, and we realize the great technical skill involved, quite apart from the sheer beauty of melody and harmony.

Even the simple outlines of the main subject of the Rondo in op. 42 provide an interesting variety of form, as the bass line quoted in Ex. 25 shows.

Ex.25.

It appears to commence in C, but the cadence in bar 4 lightly indicates that we are in A minor, but then at bar 9 we seem again to be in C. It will be noted that the second phrase, from bar 5, repeats the two previous bars, although the treble line is different. This eight-bar sentence is twice repeated, with two interludes of varying length so that the form is a+b+a+c+a, the last being shortened by two bars and leading to cadential phrases. Above this the treble runs on in varied contours without a break until the end of the subject, forty-six bars in all.

Harmonic progression also plays an important part in shaping short phrases and linking them together. The 'andante molto' of the E flat Sonata commences with two-bar phrases each with a cadence, the variety of which debars any sense of finality just as the melodic outline debars monotony. The cadences are—tonic, dominant, submediant, mediant, subdominant and dominant in the key of G minor, and in some cases the movement of the parts suggests a momentary shift of key. An extended cadence from the A flat Adagio in the C minor Sonata has already been quoted (Ex. 5, p. 17). It has an effect of shifting perspective, such as occurs in filming when the camera is moved, and four bars later there is a similar cadential phrase with different chording which is again followed by a phrase in A flat. Six others of these occur during the movement, three of them in the coda. In this the first is in F minor, the second in the same key as Ex. 5 but high up in the treble, and the third is in G minor in the bass but harmonically a semitone lower. They are all adjacent and the last one is followed by a phrase on an unresolved dominant seventh on E, and after a rest the closing bars enter immediately on the home key of A flat; as beautiful a collection of tonalities as one could wish to hear in half a dozen bars.

As Schubert's genius was so largely melodic it is not to be expected that he would experiment very much in metrical rhythms. His melodies were often so spontaneous that they carried their own rhythms and he had no need to invent them. Hence in the song-like sections and movements the basic metre is often simple and variety is attained by a complex harmonic structure that itself supplies rhythmic progress. One has only to look at most of the Impromptus to see even up to seven pages with the same figured accompaniment that is somewhat monotonous and unoriginal at a casual glance but yet full of interest for the ear and analytical mind. It is not often that one finds so complicated a rhythm as that in the 'con moto' of op. 53 where the simple opening melody is developed as below (Ex. 26c).

Ex. 26.

Yet most of the movement revolves round the initial phrase, for it occurs in so many rhythmic and harmonic transformations.

Schubert's skill in development is greater than is sometimes acknowledged. The first movement of op. 42 is a case in point. The close connexion between the first and second subjects has already been noted, but one writer states that there is no second subject, as the C major section is merely a split theme derived from previous material. On its publication in 1826 a very favourable review in the Leipzig *Allgemeine Musikalische Zeitung* considered the form so free that it was really a Fantasy and only entitled a Sonata because of the general form of the whole work. The 'Wanderer' Fantasy itself is a masterpiece of development. This also may be said to have no second subject for the E major section is derived from the opening theme and also gives rise to the E flat section. There is also a close thematic connection between the 'movements' (including the Trio section), so that the whole work may be considered as a miniature music drama constructed on a few basic interlinked themes.

IV

THE SONATAS

THE sonata with all its ramifications was the outstanding form in the latter half of the eighteenth century. It ranged from works for solo pianoforte to those for full orchestra. It has maintained its eminence up to the present time in chamber and orchestral works but has declined in the form of piano sonata, although in Beethoven's time this was considered almost as important as the symphony. Both Mozart and Haydn wrote many solo sonatas and although some of them are great works it was Beethoven who raised this form to parity with the quartet and symphony. After this there was a general decline, and although later composers produced sonatas for the piano and another instrument which more than hold their own, their solo sonatas are few and comparatively little known. Schumann reviewed very many of these works in the *Neue Zeitschrift für Musik*, and in a general article in 1839 wrote that:

It is remarkable that those who write sonatas are generally unknown men; and it is also strange that the older composers . . . cultivate this form the least. It is easy to guess the reason why the former class, generally consisting of young artists, writes them; there exists no better form in which they can introduce themselves and please the higher class of critics, therefore most sonatas of this kind may be regarded as studies in form; they are seldom the result of an irresistible inward impulse. There is, doubtless, a reason why the older composers no longer write sonatas; we leave others to guess what this reason may be. . . . It looks as if this form had lived through its vital course according to the order of things; for we cannot repeat the same form for centuries, and yet deliberate on new ones. So let sonatas or fantasias (what's in a name?) still be written, but let not music be forgotten meanwhile, and the rest will follow, with the protection of one's good genius.[1]

Composers preferred the larger forms, larger only in that they were written for two or more instruments so that more colour and variety could be introduced. This was a natural outcome of the desire for bigger emotive expression but at the same time it has restricted the individual pianist's library of great sonatas and he may well envy the violinist's increased repertoire in this form. It appears that although composers in the last century and a half have been prepared to emulate Beethoven in his chamber music and in the symphony they have not wished, or at any rate have not had the ability, to do so with the sonata for pianoforte.

Hence the sonatas of Schubert assume an added interest and importance as practically the last great works in this form, for three of his finest were composed the year after Beethoven died. Whereas Mozart wrote seventeen, Haydn about fifty, and Beethoven thirty-two, Schubert commenced twenty-three and finished only thirteen. These were produced between 1815 and 1828, that is from the age of eighteen to his death, which is a period roughly equivalent to that between Beethoven's first work and his op. 31, and gives us some indication of Schubert's immense progress in so short a period. In

[1]*Music and Musicians*, trans. Fanny Raymond, second series 1880, p. 259.

1816 the important Sonata in E known as th
Klavierstücke appeared and in the next year h
considerable time on similar works. It was nati ___, in
not inevitable, that he should take the great works of
his predecessors as models, and it is particularly significant that nearly all his early first movements open with
brief themes based on the tonic and dominant such as
are so familiar to us in the works of Haydn, Mozart and
Beethoven.

But his inspiration did not really function in this
manner. He was skilled enough to make all the necessary
motions but not able to imbue them with his own spirit.
Being essentially lyrical he liked to blossom forth immediately he put pen to paper. Although he was an expert
at handling short pregnant themes and by this method
set the inevitable tone to many a song, yet his works in
sonata form are generally most convincing when they
commence with fairly long melodic phrases which provide thematic fragments for later development. Hence
of the fourteen early sonatas, only five of which were
finished, the first and last are the most satisfactory both
in substance and form, the first being the one mentioned
above and the last the well-known op. 120 in A major
which was composed in 1819 a short time after the
'Trout' Quintet.

Even as a boy Schubert could compose fluently and
impart individuality to his music but naturally he had
not a great deal of importance to express at that early
age unless prompted by the ideas and emotions in the
poetry he so eagerly set to music, so that when he
attempted 'absolute' music he had to follow in the foot-
steps of his predecessors and let his sense of beauty

elaborate his formal structure. He had to wait for experience to mature and had to pass through a strenuous self-training, and although his genius could cover the ground in a much shorter period than that required by more slowly developing composers, yet trouble and toil still had to be undertaken. This we may judge by the details in the following table.

Year	Sonata[1]				D No.
1815	No.	1	(1) in E ⎱	both incomplete and of	157
		2	(2) in C ⎰	minor interest	279
1816		3	in E	the *Fünf Klavierstücke*	459
		4	in E minor—a fragment (quoted by Maurice Brown)—		
1817		5	(6) in A minor—op. 164		537
		6	(3) in A flat—incomplete		557
		7	(4) in E minor—published as a whole in 1948		566
		8	in D flat—incomplete but finished in E flat		567
		9	(7) in E flat op. 122—transposed and completed from no. 8		568
		10	in F sharp minor—fragment		570—1
		11	(5) in B major—op. 147		575
1818		12	in C major—fragment		613
		13	in F minor—fragment		625
1819		14	in C sharp minor		655
		15	(10) in A major—op. 120		664
1823		16	(8) in A minor—op. 143		784

[1] This list is numbered according to Maurice Brown. Numbers in brackets are those of the *Gesamtausgabe*. Most practical editions include only nos. 5, 9, 11, 15, 16, 17, 19, 21, 22, 23 and occasionally 20.

1825	17 (9) in A minor—op. 42	845
	18 in C major—'Reliquie' (unfinished)	840
	19 (11) in D major—op. 53	850
1826	20 (12) in G major—op. 78	894
1828	21 (13) in C minor	958
	22 (14) in A	959
	23 (15) in B flat	960

Before considering these works in detail a brief reference to their general background may be useful. The earlier composers were concerned rather with the form of their work but with Beethoven the music became much more an expression of the composer's personal emotions. This does not deny our obvious impression that the earlier masters did really express themselves and stamped their work with their own individuality, but emphasizes the fact that in the later period the composer was much more concerned with his own feelings and manipulated his material more from that point of view. Although there may be no real distinction in the ultimate results the change of emphasis in the mind of the composer is indicated by the fact that while Haydn and Mozart were content to let their music speak for itself and confined their directions to matters of tempo, Beethoven even in his first quartets used such expressions as 'affettuoso ed appassionata' and *La Malinconia* and gave several of his works emotive titles and later increased this use of terms to indicate definite moods, thereby showing his increasing preoccupation with the intent of his music, and this is the reason for his expansion of sonata form and the general enlargement of the entire sonata structure.

Schubert in his conception of 'absolute' music followed the older masters in theory but not in essence. The extraordinary number of 'mood' directions to be found in his songs is absent from the piano music although there is therein a far greater range of individual emotion than is to be found in that of his predecessors. He considered these moods to be self-evident in the music and gave only one work an informative title. This was the 'Tragic' Symphony and as it is not truly tragic he may have used the title for publicity purposes—which future events have justified to some extent. But there are deeply tragic passages in several of his works and one has the impression that he was more self-revealing in his sonatas than either Haydn or Mozart. The fact that he followed Beethoven in using the scherzo more often than the minuet indicates a more boisterous mood than was usual in the earlier classical period, and the tempestuous episodes in several of the slow movements show a greater depth of emotional force between the crests and troughs of sound.

From the previous list it will be noted that only four sonatas in numbers 1 to 13 were completed (excluding no. 7 for the present). Of the others, numbers 1, 2, 4, 6, 8, 10, 12 all commence with a short theme, which it has been suggested was not congenial to Schubert's style, although he finished no. 8 almost immediately in the transposed version of no. 9. Both were marked by him as Sonata II, and the previous one (no. 7 in E minor) was numbered I and then cancelled by Schubert himself (see D.566). Add to these details the fact that no. 5 was published as the *Siebente Sonate*, no. 16 as *Première grande Sonate*, no. 17 as *Letzte Sonate*; that he wrote

IV *Sonata* at the head of no. 19, and *Sonata* III on the final version of no. 22, and we realize the muddle that dogged any early study of his works as a whole, and the final fact (see footnote on p. 60) that there are virtually only fourteen sonatas even when nos. 3, 7 and 18 are included.

The *Fünf Klavierstücke* were so called in the first edition of 1843, but in 1930 a part of the MS. was discovered and found to be entitled *Sonate*. Although so early a work it is surprising how many of Schubert's most characteristic finger-prints it contains. The first subject is in E, the second in B, but the development closes in the key of the subdominant so that the reprise is practically all a fourth higher than the exposition. The core of the first subject is contained in the two first bars and although the harmonies are tonic and dominant the phrase itself is a melodic one. This is repeated a tone higher on dominant and tonic chords, and extended to lead to a more elaborate statement of the subject, with a different extension, which contains in bars 14-15 a falling figure in the tenor to become of importance in the transition, the second subject and the codetta.

Ex. 27.

The bass of the second subject at bars 33-35 with its diatonic rise from B to G sharp is noteworthy as showing Schubert's delicate harmonic sense, as is the gloomy touch in bar 42 which repeats in the minor the previous major bar, and then bursts forth on a cadence in E which is followed by powerful reiterated chords of C sharp major.

The development is confined closely to the opening theme for seventeen bars and then a short passage leads to the restatement with the first eight bars omitted. It begins a fourth higher but then drops an octave and rises again, and finally drops to bring in the second subject a fifth lower than in the exposition. This analysis has been somewhat detailed in order to prove how concise Schubert could be, and what a mastery of form he had at the age of eighteen. Here are several devices such as the major-minor fluctuations and the use of chromaticisms which already stamp his work with individuality, and his method of restatement rebuts the charge that he often brought his first subject in the reprise in the subdominant because he relished the prospect of having nothing to alter in the transition passage. It is true that there is no alteration in that particular section but the mere fact that the first subject is partly higher and partly lower than before gives it a freshness that is not possible with the ordinary formula. This change, which is found in various other sonatas, may be credited to Schubert as an innovation, for although he was not the first to use it he showed how much it can add variety without disturbing balance and permits of two keys in the reprise instead of the usual tonic key.

The other numbers in this work are just as original and delightful, several quotations having already been given. The first Scherzo is remarkable in a simple first movement form. It is in the same key as the previous movement but contrast is obtained by its suggestion of G sharp minor in the opening bars, and the subject closes in B major after a strong denial of a previous E major by minor chords on E and B. The new subject is highly chromatic with strong appoggiaturas on most of the first beats. This is followed by a short development section, after which the reprise follows the normal course. It is a powerful work quite different from any previous scherzo, and the flying octaves with their many accidentals resemble a page from a work by Chopin.

The Adagio is in C major but nevertheless it has an air of tender pathos or solemn reverie. Einstein says that Schubert meant this as an Andante, but in view of the mood the slower it is taken the better. After the opening noted on p. 18 there is a change to C minor and then an emotional rise to E flat, followed by a lovely little lead-in to a variation of the first subject in tonic and tonic minor, and then the C minor subject appears in C major, all treated in the most delicate style.

It has been suggested that the second Scherzo was written to take the place of the first. It is in orthodox form, the opening of the Trio being quoted in Ex. 3 on p. 15. A few bars later this theme passes through the key of B flat, the change to a major third up or down being another of Schubert's favourite key contrasts. The last movement is marked 'Allegro patetico' and is about the only piano work with a definite indication of mood. The word 'patetico' is not very definite in itself but the music suggests that it is used in reference to pathos as an expression of strong deep feeling. It abounds in quintuplets and sextuplets and is a highly original piece of writing.

The only criticism one can make on the work as a whole is that it lacks cohesion between the movements. The fact that the slow movement is in the key of the flat submediant does not rule it out of place, for Schubert used this key contrast as often as he did that of a minor third, and there is a change of key from E to C in the last movement. But although the movements are entirely satisfactory they do not seem to belong to one another in a way that we have been led to expect from the great sonatas. This relationship was gradually developed. At first it was confined to key in the early suites and sonatas, and the natural practice was to make the movements otherwise as different as possible. But as the composer would generally write a whole work consecutively an unconscious background would produce a certain accordance between its separate parts. However, many sonatas lack this cohesion and it was not until the time of Beethoven and Schubert that it was considered a necessity.

That this was the case in the works of Mozart and Haydn was gratefully accepted, but not considered essential, and it was not until after Schubert's 'Wanderer' Fantasy that composers thought of connecting the movements by means of a basic theme or quotations. Hence we may conclude that although Schubert in his early period could produce sonata movements to his (and our) satisfaction, he was still grappling with the problem of the work as a whole. The fact that he wrote two Scherzos and that it has been suggested that the Andante in A (D604) might be another attempt at a slow movement,[1] goes to prove that neither the composer nor his

[1] Maurice Brown, *Schubert, A Critical Biography*, p. 70.

critics were entirely satisfied with the work from this
point of view.

Nine months later Schubert became more orthodox
and less engaging in the production of the A minor
Sonata which was published in 1852 as op. 164. It is in
three movements and, except for the main subject of its
Allegretto, has not the melodic charm of the previous
work. Its form is compact and full of interest and the
harmony often unexpected. It opens in A minor with a
brief subject of two contrasting sections of 3+2 bars,
the first in full chords and the second in arpeggios of
the chord of the dominant eleventh. These five bars are
then repeated, but by an enharmonic change of G sharp
to A flat the arpeggio figure becomes a ninth on G
natural. A brief modulatory passage based on the opening phrase passes through various keys and leads to the
second subject in F which is freely developed, and to a
codetta based on a falling phrase of D flat to C which
occurs in the tenor part of the second subject. This
phrase also forms most of the development with a
similar appoggiatura effect, and is lengthened in the A
flat section to form the more melodic phrase of Ex. 28.

Ex.28.

In fact, it underlies most of the movement. Occasionally
it is inverted, sometimes it is altered to a tone, but

generally is used merely as an appoggiatura as in Ex. 28.
A few bars later where, at the beginning of the development it becomes C-B flat, B flat-A flat, A flat-G flat, F
sharp-E, and so on down to C, we meet it in sequence.
In the reprise the first subject appears in the subdominant, a fourth higher and *fortissimo* instead of piano,
and the second subject is in A major which is a third
higher than its original appearance, and, as in the
previous work, additional interest is provided by such
key relationships without departing from the basic
structure.

The slow movement opens with a beautifully balanced
subject in which melody and harmony are one in a true
Schubertian style. The sixth chord may be a dominant
ninth to the cadence in B, but to insert a bottom F sharp
would ruin the passage, and the treble G sharp to F sharp
against a bass of A sharp and A natural at bar 12 may
look harsh but does not sound so. These sixteen bars well
illustrate the composer's genius in the management of a
bass line that not only supports the melody but has a
delightfully varied contour through the inversions which
give a sense of new chords. The passage is too long for
quotation, but note the rise of A, A sharp, B at the end
of the first phrase altered to A, B, E at the next; note the
A of bar 13 falling a seventh, and if we play the passage
with any other bass notes we shall realize how inevitably
right Schubert was. This melody recurs twice in varied
form, but the intervening episodes are not inspired in
the same way, and the concluding movement is interesting merely as piano music.

The history of the E minor Sonata is very complicated,
and the four movements were not published together

until 1948. The first movement only appeared in the *Gesamtausgabe*, the Allegretto in 1907, and the Scherzo in 1928 as a supplement to *Die Musik*. The Rondo was published with an introductory Adagio adapted from an unfinished sonata as op. 145, no. 2 in 1847. The Allegretto, which is by far the best movement, has been compared with that in Beethoven's op. 90, also in E major, and indeed there are many superficial similarities, especially in the opening melodies which both dwell lovingly on the major third. Beethoven commences with a four-bar sentence and repeats it; this is answered with one of eight bars in the dominant, which is repeated, to lead back to the tonic. Schubert reverses this by opening with an eight-bar sentence answered by four bars, both repeated. Beethoven maintains his key in the first sentence but Schubert colours his cadences, going to F sharp minor at bar 4 and to B at bar 8. In the second sentence occurs a lovely little sequence, typical of the composer:

Ex.29.

But indeed the whole movement abounds in such felicitous passages, as does the Rondo which is in the same key.

The opening of this, like that of the Allegretto, hovers between the tonalities of tonic and dominant keys and then proceeds into the dominant with elusive harmonies.

A more energetic section follows, with an arpeggio bass (Ex. 30a) which later becomes melodic (Ex. 30b) and then 'Trout-like' to accompany the returning subject (Ex. 30c).

Ex.30.

Even though the Sonata as a whole is neglected, it is a wonder that these two movements have not become well known and indeed popular.

The E flat Sonata consists of four movements and is an ambitious work with much more of the Schubertian fire. It opens with a theme on the notes of the tonic and dominant chords and after a short bridge passage this is repeated with accompaniment in the tonic minor and is used as a modulatory passage to B flat and a new subject, this time melodic. This is modified and taken up by the bass where it modulates freely, commencing in D flat. Both subjects are used for the codetta so that practically the whole of the exposition is taken up by development of the subjects. As it is a hundred and

twelve bars in length the development section proper
is given over to new material which has some slight
connexion with an arpeggio figure from the codetta.
There are several alterations in the reprise, the chief of
which is the omission of the tonic minor section, but
otherwise it follows a normal course of commencing in
the tonic and modulating accordingly.

The Andante molto is a much richer movement. It
opens quite simply with two-bar phrases with charming
varieties of cadence, and the first twelve bars are repeated
with melodic elaborations and a cross-accent in the
accompaniment. Further extended, this leads to a
strongly emotional subject alternating between bass and
treble with triplet accompaniment and then a variation
of the first subject so that the whole is in A—B—A—B
form concluding with a quotation of bars 20-26 and a
brief coda of six bars. The next movement is a Menuetto
famous for its Trio, which also appears in a separate
Scherzo with two slight alterations (see p. 111). There
the two sections are in contrast, but in this sonata there
are several obvious hints of the Trio in the dotted quaver
phrases in both halves of the Menuetto.

The Finale in E flat is lyrical in a free first movement
form, the two main subjects being allied in metre but not
in expression, and the free fantasia section is in contrast
with these.

The movement commences with a four-bar sentence
which contains two germinal phrases (Ex. 31a) that
permeate the whole Allegro, and this is answered by ten
bars of delightful three- and four-part writing in the
treble, modulating to the dominant minor. This new
subject is allied to the opening by the phrases which

occur in the first and fifth bars (Ex. 31b). It is very
extended and at last leads to a tonic close (da capo)
and on to a very beautiful subject in C flat. This long
melody alternates about every nine bars (see p. 52)
between treble and tenor, and one feels that this section
should be marked 'più lento' in order to bring out its
lovely phrases with true expression. It is like a Nocturne
by Chopin. The reprise is modified considerably in key
and modulation and the whole concludes with a brief
reference to the opening bars before the final cadence.

The Sonata in B, op. 147, opens in a very tempestuous
manner with alternating phrases of forte and pianissimo
ranging through the keys of B, C sharp minor, and C
natural in the first fifteen bars. Its main theme is built
on the notes of the tonic chord but this quickly assumes
a more melodic form when the key signature changes
to G major. That does not mean much, as it merely
covers a series of modulatory sequences leading to a
new key of E major in which the work settles down for
a short time on a new subject. The signature changes

again to the home key and develops fragments of the second subject, but this is nearly all in F sharp and so leads to the double bar and repeat. The development opens very passionately and is based on the opening theme with very widely spaced leaps in either hand which gradually subside until the reprise bursts forth in the subdominant. The various key changes follow this shift and so the second subject is in A but its conclusion modulates differently, and by moving up a fourth brings it to its rightful key of B major. The whole movement looks rather chaotic but sounds well. It is unorthodox, surprisingly original and full of interest.

The slow movement is more formal, the opening eight bars in E major being answered by a bass melody with a chordal accompaniment in which chords on the half beats are 'waved' arpeggios that produce an unusual effect. There is a second section of a more strenuous character that leads gradually back to a varied recapitulation and a rather pathetic coda. The Scherzo and the Finale have their interesting points but neither fulfil the expectation held out by the previous movements nor call for special notice.

These five works have been dealt with in some detail, partly because they have hitherto been unduly neglected and also because it is these details that provide an insight into the technique that evolved into the later great sonatas. Like those of Beethoven's first period, they display the intellectual character of the musician without the deep significance that permeates the later ones. They are the product of vigorous experimental youth in which depth of feeling has not yet ripened to full expression. In spite of their individuality they are essays in craftsmanship and prepare by their amazing skill in musical presentation the foundation for the following works in which a fuller realization of life and a deepened emotional response to its joy and tragedy could be perfectly expressed by the facility thus gained. We do not expect most of the early works of a composer to be often performed, but we lose our sense of proportion if we do not know them and hear them occasionally. We have to choose between being like the person who cherishes a few choice blossoms and the enthusiastic gardener who knows how the plants develop and arrive at perfection, and by that knowledge feeds his own interest and appreciation.

After this sudden spurt in 1817 two years elapsed before another complete Sonata was produced. This was in A major, op. 120, and it has always been a favourite work. Its three movements are lyrical and concise and breathe of the open air and countryside that Schubert so loved and depicted in his brook music and such songs as 'Im Frühling' and many other spring songs. It is a happy work and the few minor passages serve merely as shadow to sunlight. The music has a translucence that had rarely been heard before and which puts it in a category by itself, and this has been attained by continued and ever changing melody which often shimmers with chromatic harmony. The form of the first movement is simple and orthodox. In the reprise the alteration of a couple of bars in the modulating episode serves to bring the second subject into the tonic. Even the codetta is repeated and after a bar rest there follows a simple final reference to the opening phrase in tender conclusion.

The slow movement is a song without words suggesting in its opening bars 'Die Sterne', and the frequent occurrence of an appoggiatura gives a meditative air to the movement. There are several points of interest such as the variation in the accompaniment to the opening melody when it recurs so that the phrase is echoed by the left hand; the movement in the treble to bring the major third into prominence a few bars before this; and the Neapolitan sixth that casts a shadow eleven bars before the end but is brightened two bars later as the major third of the key appears in the bass, although it is echoed in the melody three bars from the end. This touch of melancholy serves to heighten the happiness of the concluding movement which is in a free sonata form producing a varied interest as the two main subjects appear under various guises interspersed with brilliant runs and arpeggio passages in continually changing harmony.

Although Schubert was to write several greater sonatas he was never again to compose such a happy one, for he had to pass through the months of agony in 1822-23 which left their mark and in their way cast a shadow over sections of his music so that his piano works revealed more depth of feeling and expressed a greater realization of the tragedies and triumphs of life. He knew these at an early age but had not experienced them deeply enough to express them in 'abstract' music. Only time or circumstance could bring that to pass, and it was the 1822 period that brought Schubert suddenly to maturity and caused him to write in his diary: 'What I produce is due to my understanding of music and to my sorrows', and to a friend that 'I feel myself the most unfortunate, the most miserable being in the world'.[1] He who had been so hopeful and uninhibited had passed through the refiner's fire and could never be the same again. The carefree op. 120 became the serenity of the Sonata in G. The promise of op. 147 was revealed in op. 143.

It was in this period that the Unfinished Symphony, the 'Wanderer' Fantasy and the Sonata, op. 143 were composed, in which the mixed feelings of hope and despair are most clearly discerned, and in which the composer's indomitable spirit is expressed. The Symphony does not go beyond the catharsis reached in the second movement but the Sonata reveals a new strength of purpose, and the Fantasy expresses the power and determination that was to carry Schubert onward in the following years.

[1]See Maurice Brown, op. cit. p. 154, or Deutsch, op. cit. p. 339, for a complete version of this letter.

V

THE LATER SONATAS

THE immense satisfaction that Schubert must have derived from composing the powerful Fantasy may have banished and vanquished the mood of the Unfinished Symphony and so prevented its completion: but he was still ill when less than three months later he composed the Sonata in A minor, op. 143. His changed state of mind may be observed by comparing the opening of this work with that of the 'Trout' Quintet composed before his illness. Everyone knows the almost careless joy of that work with its gay preliminary flourish and the first phrase of the violin with its play around the major third, and in this Sonata we have the same opening notes in reverse followed by a phrase with the accent on the minor third. Here they are:

Ex. 32.
Trout Quintet

Sonata Op. 143.

This work was neglected for many years but is now recognized as truly great. In its clear, sometimes stark outline there is a wonderful depth of expression, its three movements expressing, in general terms, tragedy, resignation and determination.

In the first the struggle is between minor and major, not as key relationships but as a powerful expression of despair and hope. The conflict is hardly won, for the final full close in the major (fourteen bars from the end) is clouded by the following combined tonic and dominant chords, and a C sharp just before the final chords has to insist by its fortissimo and prolongation that the two forces are not quite equal and that the peace of the Andante has been attained. Even in this the muted passages murmur their constant reminder of tragedy and there is an upsurge of feeling in the clashing harmonies of the G flat section. The last movement opens in a strong but not happy mood. It has determination in its constant rising passages but the melody in F with its minor ninths is the song of one with still the tang of bitterness in his mouth, and yet concludes (in the coda) with a vigorous affirmation of strength to meet all odds.

The opening theme of the Sonata is menacing like the phrases of 'Aufenthalt' and overshadows the whole movement. It plunges into the depths immediately with its falling minor thirds (see Ex. 32) and although the following phrase endeavours to rise by inverting the notes it also falls in like manner. Even when the theme broadens out in the next bars each phrase concludes with a fall and this is further emphasized over a tremolo bass until the whole is repeated with intense pressure to lead to the modulation quoted on p. 30. The second subject is in the dominant major and brings some of the tranquillity which the opening was endeavouring to reach, but its metre is slightly uneasy, being marked thus:

Ex.33

This unrest becomes evident as the phrasing breaks up into fragments as a sort of contest between the two bars, the first assuming somewhat the character of bar 4 of the opening and working into the codetta which quotes the two opening bars in its final phrases. The development soon works up almost to a frenzy with its ever higher treble against the great downward scales, and then goes through a series of flat keys that make the reprise in the home key quite unexpected. There are several significant changes in both subjects and the coda repeats the codetta but then a diminished seventh introduces the series of falling thirds of the transition section which resolves to the chord of A major and is followed by the discords and concords described previously.

The slow movement commences with a serene rising melody, and Schubert with sudden inspiration altered the seventh note, which was at first E, to the mediant so that the following falling major third echoes the close of the previous movement. But the murmuring 'Neapolitan' turn on the tonic (marked 'sordini') hints at a sombre undercurrent, somewhat like the phrases of Beethoven's 'Geister' Trio and this little figure occurs constantly throughout the movement. The answering sentence to the first eight bars is not so peaceful because it is shortened by one bar and contains two dissonances instead of one and is followed by a mere three-bar phrase. The theme marked 'sordini' then develops into a descending passage leading to a forceful rise in D flat major (from the key of F), the melody of which is quickly broken by fierce dissonances. These resolve into C, in which key the first subject appears in the tenor with gentle persuasiveness. When the 'sordini' passage again attains prominence it leads to gentle cadences and a final quotation of the opening phrase.

The final movement, although in A minor, is the reverse of pathetic. There is a virility in the opening running passages that flings aside care when it breaks free into the wide arpeggios of B flat, and there is determination in the transition leading to the next subject. And although minor ninths occur in the melody here they are not accented, for the harmony is mainly dominant and tonic (in F and B flat), and the last ninth passes gracefully down to the tonic. The whole movement is taut in form and convincing in every phrase, and the whole work is probably the greatest of all the sonatas in expressiveness combined with beauty and a concise clarity and economy of material.

Over two years elapsed before Schubert turned again to the solo sonata and then three followed in quick succession. Two were written in April 1825 and the other in August. Of the first two one was left unfinished and is known as the 'Reliquie', the other published a few months later as op. 42. This is in A minor but without the tragic undercurrent of the previous work in that key. Its form has been analysed in Chapter II, and in spite of the fact that the first movement closes in the minor, whereas op. 143 ends in the major, it is a much more optimistic conclusion. The slow movement is a set of five variations on a happy, placid theme in C, the third being more agitated in C minor and the fourth reaching the climax in A flat and then modulating back to C for the final variation, which, although its second section commences with a big crescendo, gradually regains tranquillity so that the coda echoes the serenity of the opening bars. These form one of Schubert's finest sets of variations in freedom of form and expression. They do not cling so closely to their theme as do most of the other sets and the manner in which they are linked together gives unity to the movement.

The following Scherzo and Trio forms a comparatively large movement. It opens in A minor and any squareness of form is quickly broken by fortissimo interjections. The rhythm is based on the opening figure of two quavers and a minim and when it reaches the key of the relative major a sudden prolonged chord on A flat intervenes, and as it falls to the dominant of C it may be considered as a German sixth with a missing F sharp. The second half soon modulates to remote flat keys and later to the home key from which it enters an A major section; the whole Scherzo being full of verve and excitement. The Trio is in complete contrast, melodious and diatonic, commencing in F and closing in D minor with a little variation on the opening sentence.

The Rondo rushes on almost breathlessly with a care-free air, lightly harmonized, and it is the constant re-currence of phrases that commence in one tonality and then close indeterminately in another that gives the movement its intense vitality. Even when a phrase keeps within its key, like the rising minims, marked *ff*, in the bass, it is followed by sequences in other keys, as is the case with the big reiterated minim bars; and the later development of the figure in bar 47 rings the changes in E, G sharp, A flat and A major keys, and a similar state of affairs is found in the A major section.

The Sonata in C may have been meant to pair with that in A minor and there is a strong resemblance between the opening themes of each as may be seen by comparing Ex. 34 with Ex. 8 on p. 21.

But the first phrase has not the nervous energy, nor the second phrase the sharp tang of op. 42. The first notes reverse Schubert's usual expression of happiness with a rising major sixth, and major tonality is slightly clouded in the falling cadence which is stressed on repetition in bar 4. Hence the third bar endeavours to establish tonality as it does twice more before the transition, but the following phrase (bar 5) still suggests hesitancy with its stress on the submediant. The mood is not assured, and this becomes obvious with the arrival of the second subject. The first has almost lost its way in a long passage in the flat submediant, and then comes the transition noted on p. 32. The second subject is in the ominous key of B minor accompanied by the 'fate' rhythm in the bass (see Ex. 15, p. 33) and its melody is disjunct in a quite uncharacteristic style. It does occur later in the key of C major and the codetta sinks down to unisons on E for the repeat and to lead to the development of the first subject, commencing in A major and reaching a pianissimo cadence ten bars later. After this the first subject bursts forth fortissimo to the form of Ex. 34b, which continues for many bars, often in canon. The reprise is altered in length and key relationships, the second subject being in A minor and the coda very extended to include references to all the thematic material of the movement and closing, after a series of *fz* chords, with the second half of the opening sentence, very quietly in C major.

The mood changes with the first sentence of the following Andante in C minor which closes with a sad little cadence in C major, extended on repetition into a brief sequence in D flat, A flat and C minor. The next passage contains some ominous falling major sevenths and more emphatic use of the rising scale of the first sentence. Although a quiet section follows, this develops with intense emotional power and it is the alternating play of these elements that makes this one of Schubert's most moving slow movements. Even in the coda there are fortissimo and pianissimo phrases in quick succession

D

and a slight rumble of the storm in the bass of the last two bars.

The Menuetto is interesting in its modulations (see p. 34) but is unfinished. The Trio is in G sharp minor and runs along so smoothly that the discords that crash into the rhythm are quite painful. It closes on its tonic with the fifth uppermost, this D sharp being repeated by the first note of the Menuetto. As this is an E flat and ascends to F a somewhat startling result is caused.

The Rondo was evidently written in one of Schubert's dull periods and is devoid of real interest. His heart was cold and probably he continued for five pages with decreasing interest, to stop in the middle of a phrase. As with the Unfinished Symphony he had exhausted himself in two movements, so here it seems more than likely that he saw the uselessness of finishing a work which had really completed its purpose without the necessity for an additional two movements.

Op. 53 in D major is the longest sonata if counted by pages. Length of performance is another matter as it depends on the tempo of each movement, and the number of bars may be misleading as, for example, the Rondo in op. 42 is in two-four time while that in op. 53 is in common time and will have only half the number of bars for an equivalent length. If the printed page is taken as a unit the following comparisons may be made:

Sonata in D, op. 53	32 pages
Sonata in G (Fantasy)	31 pages
Sonata in B flat	30 pages
Fantasy ('Wanderer')	30 pages
Sonata in A minor, op. 42	24 pages

The Sonata in D as a whole is happy and at times merry, the latter state not generally considered to be sonata-like since the time of Beethoven, although Haydn would certainly not have agreed with such an opinion. What detracts from the first and last movements to some extent is the presence of the long and short scale passages and arpeggios so much used by Schubert's minor contemporaries as a substitute for real thought, and here used rather overmuch out of pure joy of sound. It was written during that happy holiday at Gastein when deep thought gave place to sheer joyousness, and the pleasure of life amid beautiful scenery is evident throughout the work.

The first movement opens with a bold figure that shifts quickly into the region of the subdominant and then back to a restatement in D minor and keys further afield, returning with a triumphant re-entry of the opening theme and then off again to a modulatory episode comprised chiefly of runs and broken chords. The main second subject enters abruptly 'un poco più lento' in G and C to quite a different rhythm, but it might be argued that the second subject begins in the dominant at bar 40 and carries on in that key for several bars after the 'più lento' interlude. Otherwise this is another case (like op. 42) of a second subject being very short itself and having only a small part to play as it is not developed elsewhere. It is followed by an enormous codetta derived from the modulating episode; the development section is based on the first subject; and the reprise follows the usual course, the coda concluding with the opening theme extended into a more satisfying section 'un poco più mosso'.

The slow movement is in A and after the initial phrase it roams freely in various tonalities. The dynamics also change frequently so that here also there is a certain atmosphere of carefree joy. It is in rondo form but gives the impression of variations on various themes. The rhythmic basis is contained in the opening bars (see Ex. 26, p. 55) for the three quavers and dotted crotchet figure is syncopated for the following subject (Ex. 26c). The first sentence is quite regular as this rhythm carries the melody right on to its full close, but after this it is continually broken into short phrases with devious tonalities and various developments of the rhythm that present ever changing colour and pattern. The second subject follows on similar lines and its climax takes up the rhythm of the 'più lento' of the first movement.

The Scherzo with its exuberant rhythm has also highly diversified tonal variations and stresses, and the second half modulates delightfully from D to B flat where it remains for twenty-one bars, to be followed by a modification of the first section. The Trio in G is in complete contrast, its even rhythm and diatonic harmony being seldom abandoned. The major chord on the mediant occurs twice and there are sudden shifts in the middle of the movement—from C to E flat: E flat to G flat: and G flat to B minor. There is a link of ten bars to return to the Scherzo which is altered to some extent after its fortieth bar and extended by a dozen bars. Hence the three parts consist of 330 bars—118 + 72 + 140.

The Rondo is a very light-hearted movement with a slightly slower and more serious second episode of considerable length. The main subject is very simple, varied on its second appearance and still more so in its final form. The first episode is a mixture of scales and figures reminiscent of the first movement, and the whole concludes with a 'più lento' reference to the first subject, dying away to pianissimo. Each movement in its coda gives the impression of the shy Schwammerl retreating quietly into the background to allow the pianist to take all the applause, feeling perhaps that the whole work suggests gaiety without reason (except for the marvellous technical skill): a happy state of mind which we now generally lack and therefore in our hearts envy and perhaps condemn. That the last movement has been criticized as lacking the dignity necessary in the sonata is due to forming an imaginary standard of judgement to which Schubert evidently did not subscribe. The themes certainly have a childlike innocence such as is to be found in his little song 'Seligkeit' (as a brief quotation will show), and which Mahler probably had in mind when writing the last movement of his fourth Symphony, for he uses similar themes and even quotes Schubert, perhaps unconsciously.

Ex. 35.

Despite his originality in so many ways Schubert did not vary the basic form of the sonata. He kept to the

three- or four-movement pattern, never used an Introduction, and did not vary the order of the movements to
the extent that Beethoven did. What he did was to slow
down the tempo of the first movement to some extent
and the next Sonata in G commences 'Molto moderato e
cantabile' in twelve-eight time. Hence the broad phrases
of the first page do not have a 'first-movement' appearance and this may have been one reason for its publication as 'Fantasy, Andante, Menuetto and Allegretto'.
And of course Allegretto does not seem to indicate a
Sonata Finale.

Schumann was delighted with the work and it certainly shows the most lovable side of Schubert's character. It has a serenity such as we find in songs like 'Der
Sieg' and 'Das Abendrot' with their opening lines 'O
unbewölktes Leben' and 'O wie schön is deine Welt', and
like them it stresses the mediant in its prolonged chords
which change in their upper part only to give undulation
to the rhythm and re-emphasize the major third:

Ex. 36.

The first phrase is answered in the subdominant and
so keeps the mood subdued, although it closes in the
dominant (the bass is noted below the melody). The first
phrase is then repeated but with an interrupted cadence

that allows for a slight rise in expression, and the following full close in the tonic rises to the mediant again by way of A sharp. The next section is in B minor, but being over its dominant pedal there is more an impression of F sharp major, especially as the bar rhythm of the opening is slightly altered and the cadence is on the dominant to lead to a repetition in B major. This modulates beautifully back to G for a repetition of the opening bars and a slight build-up to the second subject.

This is in the dominant, ten bars in length and varied in the following ten bars. After a brief episode the codetta refers to the first subject and closes with a delightful variant in the tenor part. The development opens with the first fortissimo as it quotes the opening bar in G minor but this changes to E flat in the next bar with a rising treble that plays an important part in this section:

Ex. 37.

Both subjects are freely developed for fifty-two bars but the outstanding feature is the rising bass derived from Ex. 37 in the second bar. This is Schubert's *aufschwung* or soaring expression such as occurs at the end of 'Todtengräbers Heimweh' and in the C major Symphony, and here it negates the minor quality of some of the phrases, although the section in C minor reaches tremendous force in the *fff* bars. This climax very gradually subsides to *ppp* for the reprise in which the B minor and major section is cut and the codetta lengthened for further references to the first subject which bring the movement to a serene close.

The Adagio opens in tranquil mood, but in bars 9 and 10 there are drops of a fifth and seventh to interrupt the even flow of the melody and presage a stronger emotion. They occur in rapid succession in transition to the second subject and expand in interval in the fortissimo section to become more prominent as they develop. All this is varied on repetition and closes quietly to the strains of the opening subject without the falling intervals.

The Minuet in B minor is rather staid but full of interest and in entire contrast to the Trio which commences with a little phrase in B minor that suddenly changes to the major to carry on as a delightful melody containing an inversion of a three-note figure to be found in the cadences of the Minuet.

The first phrase of the Allegretto has an interesting rhythm as the long D seems like a pause although its length gives balance to the phrase which, with its added cadential phrase, supplies the rhythm of the whole of the first section:

Ex. 38.

Later comes a brisk quaver movement above or below rhythmic chords starting in C but passing through several keys. Eventually the first subject re-enters in the left hand and continues to a change from G to E flat. The subject in this key is itself in ternary form, the middle section being a beautiful melody in C minor with an exquisite use of the Neapolitan sixth and the major chord on the supertonic. This melody is taken up and modified by the bass, and then repeated in C major—also in treble and bass. The E flat section then returns to lead to the first subject with slight additions and a *morendo* coda concluding with the three-bar phrase, Ex. 38. It is a very long movement with light dynamics (there are only three short fortissimo passages), but the interest is maintained by the variety of form which, being roughly summarized, shows that there are really six 'subjects'.

bars 1— 55	First subject in ternary form, modulating to
55—123	episode in E leading to
124—180	first subject repeated and modulating to
181—320	episode in E flat with secondary in C minor and major—bars 212—278.
321—410	First subject and coda.

The three last sonatas were written in September 1828, only a few weeks before Schubert's death. It was a year of great masterpieces for in it were composed the 'Great' Symphony, the string Quintet, the sixth Mass, the *Schwanengesang* and two major piano duets; and the sketches of these sonatas shows that he spent much time on them. That he could complete three such different works—nearly a hundred pages of music—gives rise to the thought that he must have overworked himself almost to exhaustion and so contributed to the final collapse which a reserve of strength might have overcome.

These works may well be compared with Beethoven's last sonatas because they seem to be the final pronouncements of great minds. Of course neither knew this, and if time had permitted they would doubtless have written other sonatas. The sense of finality is with us who cannot imagine any greater succeeding works and who perceive in these a summation of the composer's output. Both had gone through trial and tribulation and the passions of sorrow and joy, and had arrived at that period when they could meditate on the inner meaning of life while still expressing its heights and depths. Schubert could still be gay but withal reflective, passionate but reserved, expansive yet cogent, still original but not experimental. Such qualities were indeed patent in the works already discussed in this chapter but these last works have still more depth of expression. The sequence of emotional thought is more highly controlled and resolved with persuasive logic.

The first of these sonatas is in C minor and has a short peremptory subject. It may be said to consist of six bars only for although it proceeds to a full close in bar 11 as the reprise also does, in the latter case there is considerable alteration even after the fourth bar, and the exposition bars 21-26 repeat the first six bars in melodic outline and bass. The subject itself is a series of staccato chords over a tonic pedal, their upper notes rising from tonic to dominant with an F sharp as an augmented sixth to the first cadence and an E natural in the third bar as though to challenge the opening C minor chord.

The second subject in the relative major is of a very flexible nature quite distinct from Schubert's vocal line. In the earlier works some of his melodies would have been suitable for verse but they became more and more instrumental in that they departed from any recognizable verbal rhythm.

The treble of this subject is given in Ex. 39 and the first four-bar phrase is poised around the A flat of a subdominant chord. The melody is then repeated in an inner part and the rise in the upper part of bar 5 is carried on two bars later, while the sequence in bar 10 suddenly introduces an unexpected key that as suddenly disappears. Hence, although flowing freely, it is a melody of interwoven thematic fragments that are able to take an important place in the movement.

The development is full of surprising key changes and overlapping tonalities. In the fifth bar the bass continues in A flat as the upper part moves to D flat and is repeated a few bars later a tone higher. Then there is a D flat chord over one in F minor, and although these may be easily explained harmonically the aural effect is that of two lines of harmony as the right and left hands pursue their way to concords in three-bar rhythm. Then comes one of Schubert's curious changes of key signature. Here it is to C major although the modulation is to A major, returning to the original three flats after fifteen bars. The bass of this section is a development in various ways, such as extension or inversion, of the phrase *a* of Ex. 39.

Ex. 39.

This is carried on for many bars until only two attenuated lines are left with a gap of five octaves between them. The right hand then carries on in chromatic runs as the left hand introduces the staccato figure of the first subject in preparation for its proper return. There is a long coda which makes much use of material from the development so that the main impression of the whole movement is one of repressed nervous energy.

The Adagio may be considered a solemn meditation on the above movement for it too has the subdominant cadence which has so often occurred and the sudden tonal changes to flat keys (see Ex. 5, p. 17). There is also an agitated second subject that steals in at first and soon subsides but is longer and much more forceful on its reappearance. It is a beautiful movement and the following Menuetto, although in C minor, brings a touch of brightness. The first phrase is one of three bars but the next is of four bars, as its initial rising phrase is extended into the unexpected tonality of A flat, and this is followed by a five-bar phrase closing in E flat. After a more vigorous contrasting section the left hand takes up the opening melody but the phrasing is broken by the insertion of two one-bar rests in surprising positions. The Trio is also delightfully phrased and deliciously harmonized.

It is the Finale that makes us realize the amount of pent-up energy in the harmonic restlessness of the first movement, for here the key-changes, about twenty in number, are spread over a broad expanse of over fourteen pages in irresistible impetuosity, and this number of keys does not take into account the modulations occurring in many sequences and transitions that flash through various tonalities. It opens in tarantella style in C minor with a quickly rising theme that soon begins to leap in octaves. At the change of key to C sharp minor the theme is a series of falling fifths, as of a 'ride to the abyss', which reaches a climax of thundering chords in E flat minor. All this is repeated and developed at great length—an outstanding feature being the frequent use of the 'Neapolitan' transition and the absence of Schubert's bright keys. Although there are the contrasts of major and minor most of the modulations are on the flat side or if upward to the sharps then in the minor mode. The only important exception is the middle episode in the key of B major, a broad melody that cannot resist passing into the rhythm of the first subject.

This movement has been compared with the finale to Beethoven's Sonata op. 31, no. 3, which is only half as long, but this does not imply that Schubert was diffuse. It can only be so if the interest flags and from a technical point of view no work can be more absorbing. In performance the continuity depends on the pianist and no music wants more careful study than this. Anyone with the necessary technique can romp through the Finale of the 'Wanderer' Fantasy and give a fairly good impression of it, but unless this one is well thought out it will lose its impelling form and appear merely as a series of episodes. Like the Finale to the C major Symphony it needs genius to interpret it for there are so many heights and depths of expression that each climax has to be carefully calculated and graduated to bring out the complete form. Only then will the picture be complete with foreground, middle and distance in proper perspective and the passage of mere time obliterated. The Beethoven Finale is Presto but this is only Allegro, and it is not speed that is wanted but an innate sense of form that can provide the feeling of velocity. A careful analysis of the song 'An Schwager Kronos' would be a good preliminary study for this movement.

Although the next Sonata in A, is so different from the above there are some striking similarities in their opening sentences. Whereas the first maintains the tonic in the bass throughout while the treble rises from tonic to dominant, in the second the treble repeats the tonic for the same number of times (fourteen notes) as the bass rises from tonic to dominant (although in a shorter period). Also both subjects have a tonic minor seventh in the third bar as though hinting at their instability. Apart from this seventh the A major subject is, in its first part, a firm six-bar statement; but the tonic cadence that seems almost inevitable because of its two-bar preparation is broken, and there follows a six-bar response of harmonic fluctuation with a three-bar lead-in to a repetition of the whole subject considerably modified. The tonic pedal is in an inner part and an additional upper part sets up harmonic clashes, while in

the response the harmonies become concordant. Hence
the two opening themes are entirely reversed in character. At first the bass rises in thirds as at Ex. 40a. On
repetition it is as Ex. 40b. In the second half of the
subject the thirds rise as at c, but are altered into the
key of A major on repetition.

Ex.40.

From these elements arises much of the ensuing movement and a whole mass of unfamiliar tonal juxtaposi-
tions. The subject begins to modulate with a falling
sequence on *d* and leads to E major for the second subject.

This is somewhat like the corresponding passage in
the 'Waldstein' Sonata, but after eight bars it modulates
to C major and then back again—to be followed by a
long passage above a bass derived from Ex. 40b. Then,
rather surprisingly, the second subject reappears with a
slight extension introducing a new melodic fragment.
This constitutes the main part of the following development section, which has only one brief reference to the

first subject. The lead-in to the reprise has been mentioned on p. 32 and then the work follows a normal course to the coda, which extends the codetta to some length with various statements of the first subject and its derivatives.

The Andantino is comparatively short and simple but wonderfully expressive. It opens in F sharp minor with a tender melody and this on repetition has a more subdued cadence. The melody is then repeated, but harmonized, not in the tonic major, but in the relative major. Although this melody occurs six times all sense of monotony is avoided by the various nuances and several extensions of phrase which produce a form of:

$$8 : 8 + 2 : 8 + 6 : 8 : 8 + 2 : 8 + 6.$$

These wistful sentences fade away in a long morendo cadence and the treble then becomes rather agitated, leading to an episode in C minor which builds up into great passionate waves of sound until a great chromatic ascent closes in C sharp minor. Then follows a series of pleading little recitatives, their tenderness denied by *fz* chords, but serenity is regained as the first subject is intimated in the tonic major. However, it enters in the original key but in more elaborate form and again gradually fades to silence.

The Scherzo is lively and gay in rhythm and key contrasts that are echoed more soberly in the Trio; but it may be noted here that in these last works there is not the light-hearted modulation up by a major third which is Schubert's expression of pure joy. In this movement the chief modulations are a minor third up (A to C in the Scherzo, D to F in the Trio), so that although the emotive force regains its strength on returning to the original key it has been lowered to some extent.

The Rondo is happy in its two main subjects. The first is a beautiful melody with a rhythm that calls to mind the felicitous phrases of 'Der Taubenpost' and 'Im Frühling', and its second sentence gives a hint of future harmonies as it slides through the major chord on the supertonic. The whole subject is repeated with the melody in the tenor, and a short transition modulates to the dominant to introduce a fresh melody. This is expanded from its first phrase, which consists of a reiterated dominant that rises by a little run up to the tonic, a thematic fragment that is much used to modulate to many different keys as the phrases build up until cascades of arpeggios enter at the ends of the bars and then in every bar. After a decrescendo only bare octave leaps are left in the treble to lead to a fresh version of the first subject. The next section is more difficult to define than to analyse. It is all based on the opening phrase which is distorted chromatically and sometimes condensed, as the following extract shows, *a* being the original melody and *b* the bass of the development:

It is a furious page and although followed by a subdued section there is a sense of foreboding when the low bass notes enter. Peace returns with the entry of the first subject in F sharp major and then in A, which recapitulates as far as the arpeggio section, and then a long silence. After this the subjects are tried out in broken fragments between empty bars as though neither could bring satisfaction, and the movement ends with a passionate 'presto' with great leaps in the last five bars.

This is really the most inexplicable of the sonatas. All the subjects are beautiful and their working out masterly, but what lies behind them seems beyond verbal expression. The changes of mood are often so sudden that it needs bar by bar analysis even to discuss them. There is the constant recurrence of the leaping octave, the great climax of the slow movement followed by recitatives, and the middle and final sections of the Rondo, all with a powerful significance that can only be absorbed. It is a joy to the ear but still more to the mind that can discern the thoughts it conveys.

Whatever the implications of this sonata, Schubert had attained serenity of mind in the next one in B flat. It opens with a subject similar in content to the Sonata in G. It too is 'molto moderato' and it rises gently to a prolonged mediant, but there is a touch of pathos in the low 'Neapolitan' trill with which it closes, although the next trill leads to a restatement a major third lower which is really in the brighter key of F sharp. The theme then becomes more agile, but leads back to the subject and then a quick transition to F sharp minor (noted on p. 29). The new subject is developed at much length and the codetta concludes with several disjunct phrases —but not with the restless spirit near the end of the previous sonata. They are rather in the manner of those cadence phrases of the slow movement of the C minor Sonata and in several of them the treble rises by semi-tones to the major third of a chord.

This is one of the few sonatas with first and second time double bars, and in this case the first is important as there is a section of nine bars concluding on a bass trill *ffz* to lead to the return. The development opens with a variation of the first subject passing through the minor keys of C sharp, F sharp and B in the course of eight bars and then linking up with a phrase from the second subject. Then the bass announces a theme as it rises on the triad and this becomes more and more important until with a key signature of two flats it takes over the main part of the next forty bars. Then the first subject appears tentatively in D minor, B flat (its original key) and D minor, as does the bass trill on the tonic at each transition and at the end to bring in the reprise. This follows the usual course but ends with a placid quotation of the first subject. The opening phrase is altered so that the tonic replaces the mediant in the upper part and this serves to bring into greater relief the mediant as the phrase is repeated with all the thirds in the upper part, and the quotation concludes with the bass trill suggesting that there are still hidden depths in the phrase.

The slow movement is in C sharp minor—a rise of a minor third—but it is not in melancholy mood. Although there are phrases that are deeply pathetic they stir the feelings with sympathy as though Schubert were expressing his compassion for humanity as he did in the 'Litanei'. Despite its simple outlines there is a noble breadth and depth of form in the long-drawn phrases and melodic movement. The first eight bars are on a tonic pedal with a persistent rhythm that governs the whole of the first part. The melody rises by degrees and not until the ninth bar does the dominant appear in a series of phrases that lead to the first climax with appoggiaturas on the strong beats. The next phrase passes in a very tender manner through the key of A to a repetition of the melody which is now harmonized in the relative major, and the second half rises still higher to the second climax with its corresponding descent. The episode in A is a song of peace and tranquillity. There are no modulations although there are three brief incursions to other tonalities. The first subject returns as before but with a little figure in the bass that with its D sharp emphasizes the key, but at bar 14 there is a sudden change to C major instead of the passing reference to A. As the chord previous to this C is G sharp (or A flat) the rise up by a major third has a most moving effect. This key remains for eight bars and then the original phrases return for twelve bars. The coda enters the tonic major in which the previous appoggiaturas are modified to suspensions.

It is a wonderful movement in great contrast to that of the previous sonata, for even its dynamics are subdued. Pianissimo is the ruling sign and the very few fortes are brief and quickly attenuated. It would seem impossible to follow such a movement without producing a severe anticlimax, but the Scherzo has a lightness and delicacy that sustains the detached and elevated sentiments aroused by the Andante. It is marked 'con delicatezza' and the melody keeps to the upper part of the keyboard almost throughout, and only appears in the bass near the end so that it may rise through two octaves. The melody is lifted by a 'passing' chord in bar 5 as the previous F is sharpened to rise to G and the subsequent use of the turn in the cadence is delightful, as are the ensuing modulations with the enharmonic change from D flat to F sharp minor and the gradual return to the home key. Although the Trio commences in the tonic minor it has a rhythmic urge to its major cadences and supplies an exquisite contrast to the happy Scherzo.

An important factor in the Finale is the long 'call' note with which it opens, always associated with the first subject. It is a long octave G and seems to announce the key of the relative minor but resolves itself into the dominant of C minor of a phrase that is itself a preliminary to the real key of B flat to which the phrase is then adapted. The next sentence is in E flat but has premonitory F sharps and does finally close in G but without the mediant. A repetition follows with the F sharp eliminated and the melody goes into A flat until it finally closes in G major (with the mediant). This first section has therefore a highly involved harmonic structure that sets a pattern for the rest of the movement.

Although generally referred to as a Rondo it has little similarity to the text book form as an outline analysis will show:

A bars	1— 32	First subject.
B bars	33— 85	First part repeated, modified and lengthened to lead to
C bars	86—153	second subject—a flowing melody in the dominant ending on a seventh, followed by two bars rest.

D bars 156—224   A fresh subject in full chords in F minor, passing through G flat minor and so to a tarantella-like section that gradually merges into the opening rhythm.

A bars 224—255   First subject.

       256—312   Development of same.

B bars 313—359   B. altered to lead to tonic.

C bars 360—427   Second subject, plus 2 bar rest.

D bars 430—490   Repetition of D.

E bars 491—540   First subject: four bars only repeated over a bass G, then G flat, then F, followed by a short Presto based on the same, and concluding with a whole bar rest in lieu of the expected long final chord.

VI

THE SMALLER PIANO WORKS

THE smaller works are far too numerous to mention in detail. There are Adagios, Andantes, Allegros, Allegrettos, Scherzos, Fugues, Marches, Minuets, Ecossaises, Polonaises, Galops and Waltzes and even a Cotillon and Albumblatt, some of which have not been published. All are of interest although few are suitable for concert performance. They are generally small and intimate effusions written for friends, or jottings of ideas, often in complete form, that might be useful in a larger work.

Of all these works the *Ländler*, *Deutsche Tänze* and *Walzer* are the most numerous. There are over fifty numbers in the Deutsch catalogue and as these may consist of anything from one to thirty-eight items there are over five hundred individual waltzes spread over the years from 1812 to 1827. There seems to be little or no difference in the form of these dances, and some of them are labelled indifferently. Most consist of two eight-bar sections, each repeated, but in some Schubert anticipated the later waltz form by extending this framework in various ways. One has two bars of preparatory bass, some have the repetitions written out with different endings, and some have Trios. For instance, no. 5 of the *Letzter Walzer* consists of sixteen and twenty-eight bars, and so does the Trio, and as each section is to be repeated and a da capo sign observed there are two hundred and

twenty bars in all. For the twelve *Deutsche Tänze*
(D420) Schubert provided a big coda of a hundred and
twelve bars.

There is a good chance that many of these were
played impromptu by Schubert at friendly gatherings
and written down afterwards, and that when an oppor-
tunity ocurred for publication he added to them in
order to complete a set. However, each is perfect in itself
and the grouping, sometimes by similarity and at others
by contrast either in form or key, is quite delightful.
Some may even be considered as miniature studies as,
for example, op. 18, no. 6 which opens with a Schuman-
nesque rhythmic figure: no. 12 which has reiterated
triplets on the third beat: op. 9, no. 33 with two
quavers on the first beat of each bar; and op. 127, no.
6 which has long scale passages in the bass while its
Trio consists of a quaver chord and rest on every beat.
Op. 50, no. 30 opens with a simple phrase but the
second half is quite boisterous with its great leaps and
cross-accented bass.

Ernest Newman suggested in semi-humorous vein that
the waltz might outlast the more solemn forms of music
and although he gave full credit to Schubert for his
work in this field he said also that he never enlarged the
'rhythmic and harmonic ideas to the extent we might
have expected—the best seem to cry aloud for further
development—for which some of them had to wait the
coming of Liszt'. But Liszt adapted them for concert
purposes whereas Schubert was writing for dancers.
Brahms also had a musical public in mind when composing the *Liebesliederwälzer* while Schubert's idea was
to satisfy a dancing public, and in these circumstances

it is surprising what interest he could instil in the rigid eight-bar sentences.

At any rate the suggestion that there is any lack of harmonic ideas may be readily disproved by examination. In the second half of op. 9, no. 2 Schubert modulates from A flat minor to E major and back again in the space of five bars: no. 14 shifts from D flat to A and back: no. 32 from F to D flat and back; and no. 33 similarly from F to A flat. There is nothing especially notable about these modulations with Schubert but their charm lies in the ease with which the melody flows on through these transitions in so few bars. Often there are sequences such as that in op. 18, no. 2, where the chord following a close in D sharp adds a seventh and drops to G sharp, and then adds a seventh to this and falls to F sharp minor. No. 2, op. 9 (mentioned above) commences happily in A flat, but the first phrase is answered in sequence a semitone higher. The first sentence has four leaning notes on the down beats and the second sentence has them in every bar which produce a wistful impression that caused the publisher to give it the title of *Trauerwalzer*. The first of the *Deutsche Tänze* (D366) opens with a light-hearted sequence descending in tones. The ninth begins with full chords in B minor and concludes the first half with Ex. 42a. This is taken up immediately in the next bar by Ex. 42b and four bars later it enters in the bass, and then in the treble as at Ex. 42a to conclude.

Very many quotations could be made to illustrate the charm of these little works which provided a happy hunting ground for the arranger of *Lilac Time*, and it is a pity that pianists have not taken a like liberty. There is nothing sacrosanct about their present arrangement. Few people would wish to play or listen to twenty or more waltzes straight off. Their practical use has disappeared and we are left with a vast number of individual gems which could be selected and formed into small groups. Such would provide an intermezzo or pleasant introduction or conclusion to the usual piano recital, and there

Ex.42.

is no doubt that many amateur pianists who are not sufficiently interested to procure the whole of the dances would be delighted to obtain albums containing half-a-dozen or so selected numbers.

The same may be said of the other dances which are all lively and interesting. There are about fifty minuets most of them with trios, which perhaps should not be considered as dance music, but the first group of these is especially interesting for the following reason. It consisted of twelve minuets and trios written in 1812. It was shown to Mozart's friend Dr. Anton Schmidt who said that the young composer would become 'a master such as there have been few as yet'.[1] Unfortunately these works were lent so often to various friends that they were lost and we have no knowledge of what the good Doctor saw. The Ecossaises and Galops are all very short numbers in two-four time and do not allow for much elaboration.

The other small compositions are spread over the years, especially from 1813 to 1818. Some are unfinished and others of slight interest, and most of them were probably attempts to complete the various unfinished sonatas. The Menuett (D600) to which Brown gives the date 1814 instead of 1818 is the only piano work of that year. It has a stately 'pizzicato' bass and some delicate phrasing with a middle section that develops the descending passage in the previous cadence. D610 is a Trio in E which Deutsch suggests belongs to this Menuett and was rewritten by Schubert in 1818 'for his dear brother'. It is inscribed thus as a 'Trio to be considered as the lost son of a Menuett'.

The *Albumblatt* is a much later composition, written in 1825 in the birthday book of Anna Hönig whose family were very friendly with Schubert. He wrote several such mementos, and this one shows how original his mind was, even impromptu. It is only a sixteen-bar piece but is delightful in its phrasing, the first cadence with the chords of C sharp minor, D and G, and the harmonies of the second half. No tempo is given but it has a meditative air somewhat like the song 'Himmelsfunken' and does not sound like a 'Walzer' as it is called in the Deutsch catalogue.

The Adagio (D505) is known generally as part of op.

[1] O. E. Deutsch, op. cit. p. 880.

145 but it belongs to the incomplete Sonata in F minor
and was written in D flat.[1] It was shortened, transposed
to E and adapted to form an introduction to the Rondo
in E which is itself a movement from the E minor sonata
of 1817. It is a pity this was done, although the Adagio
in its spurious form certainly serves admirably as an
introduction to the following melody that is the chief
charm of the Rondo. This occurs four times but on the
second and fourth times in the unusual keys of G and C
and in the varied form of Ex. 30c, p. 70. The second
subject (Ex. 30b) commences in G sharp minor but goes
to B, and on repetition commences in C sharp minor and
thence to E. Despite this wide variety of keys the long
modulating episodes that make much use of the bass of
the opening bar also range widely in their harmonies.

The Adagio in E (D.612) is a fine movement and has
something of the rhapsodic form of the Allegro of the
Fünf Klavierstücke. After the calm opening sentence it
becomes very restless with long chromatic runs and
chords, and when the main subject recurs it is very much
elaborated. It may have been intended for the unfinished
Sonata in C, composed at the same time, and one can
hear in it 'the growing discontent and unhappiness of
the composer in the early months of 1818'.[2]

The two Scherzos are fine works although short as
individual solos. The first is an Allegretto in B flat,
delicate fairy-like ballet music in which much use is
made of the opening triplet figure. The middle section
has one of Schubert's favourite modulations to the flat

---

[1] Even in a late recording of this sonata by Friedrich Wierhrer
the Adagio has not been restored to its proper place.
[2] Maurice Brown, op. cit. p. 78.

submediant as the triplet motif leads from F to D flat
and its dominant and subdominant chords. The Trio
forms a placid contrast. The second Scherzo is 'Allegro
moderato' in D flat. It is shorter and more vigorous with
a sudden modulation that wrenches the key to E major
(see p. 35), which repeats the opening phrase and then
proceeds to a series of sequences with a graceful melodic
line. The Trio has a lilting rhythm of five-bar phrases
exquisitely formed and is a slightly different version of
that used in the E flat sonata of the same year (1817).
The March written in the following year is studded with
striking modulations in spite of its shortness. Starting in
E, its first phrase passes to F sharp minor and the next
passes through C, and abrupt changes rapidly follow.
The Trio in contrast moves evenly over a steady staccato
bass and the varying tonalities are graceful rather than
startling.

The *Moments Musicaux*, although published in two
books in 1828, were not all composed in the same period.
At least two of them were written much earlier and
first published in two issues of a *Musical Album*, no. 3
as *Air Russe* in 1823 and no. 6 as *Plaintes d'un Troubadour* a year later. Deutsch places the composition of them
all in 1823 (D780) but Brown suggests November of
1827 as the dates for nos. 1, 2, 4 and 5. They are nearly
all in ternary form but quite different from each other in
style, texture and content.

The first is in C minor and the first part consists
mainly of development of the opening phrase, Ex. 17a
p. 39, sometimes below the chording of the fourth bar,
once in canon and in one place appearing rather angrily
on a B major chord. The middle section commences in D

with a sentence of 2 + 2 + 3, and although the bass is in triplets it is really a varied dominant pedal below a two-bar sequence and then in one-bar sequence over a similar pedal in G.

The second number is an Andantino in A flat akin to Schubert's moonlight and barcarolle songs in its two subjects. The first opens with full chords with a gradually increasing rhythmic movement:

Ex.43.

It will be noted that there are first two short similar phrases and then a sort of fusion that extends the sentence up to E flat and so forms a four-bar sentence. The phrase is then lowered to the tonic minor with a prolonged cadence of three bars, and then stated in E flat minor to rise to a climax on top G flat. All this is repeated with slight but telling modifications to close on D flat. The following melody is the 'poised' type in F sharp minor (Ex. 43a) with movement delayed to the third bar, and the lack of a cadence in the fourth allows the sentence to be prolonged by another two bars with still further melodic movement. The whole is repeated and extended to eight bars and a brief transition brings back the main subject in A flat. This also is altered and extended, its final phrases containing more than a hint of the coda to the first movement of the G major sonata (of 1827). As the work is in a—b—a—b—a form the F sharp minor melody returns and concludes with one of Schubert's most tender minor-major transformations, and so to the final appearance of the first subject.

No. 3 in F minor is so well known that observations are unnecessary except to note the elaborate coda. The form is ternary, 8 + 16 + 8, with repeats, but then there follow 20 bars of delightful playing with the theme, with piquant harmonies and a final cadence in the tonic major.

The fourth, in C sharp minor, is a kind of moto perpetuo. There are only two parts, a legato semiquaver treble and a staccato quaver bass, and it looks like Bach but sounds like Schubert as various forms of his favourite harmonies appear. In the latter half the bass becomes melodic and legato and closes on a dominant seventh followed by an empty pause bar. The middle section then enters in the tonic major (D flat = C sharp), in utter contrast with full harmony and well defined sentences. There is an air of whimsical gaiety in the rhythm as the accent is thrown forward in every bar and what appears like an anacrusis comes on the first beat:

Ex.44.

There are various modulations and the second half commences in what can only be called the extreme key of F flat major. The first subject is repeated entire, including

the pause rest. Then comes the coda—two bars of the
second subject in D flat and two bars of the first in C
sharp minor—as much as to say in jocular mood 'Well,
here were the two melodies. Do you like them?'

The opening of no. 5 has been mentioned on p. 38.
It is an extremely vigorous work and the only variation
of the crotchet-and-two-quaver metre occurs at the main
cadences, the four climactic fortissimo chords and a short
middle section that has four quavers to the bar. The
power of the work depends not only on continuous
staccato and the emphasis on nearly every first beat but
to the formation of chords and the leaping of their parts,
together with the alternation of concords and discords
that begin various phrases. The work concludes in the
tonic major with alternate *piano* and *fortissimo* bars,
and a final bar rest to take the place of a final chord.

Varied references have been made to the last number.
The publisher's title of 'A troubadour's lament' is inade-
quate to describe this passionate work. Although it is
mainly in four-bar phrases the rhythm is very irregular
and the harmonies unusual. The very opening is a cry
of pain and the retarded cadence of bar 7 is agonizing.
The next sentence ends pathetically and this feeling is
carried on to the E major section (mentioned on p.19).
The constant vacillation between anguish and pathos is
one of the wonders of this Allegretto and gives it a place
with the last songs. The Trio is calm but the underlying
emotion lurks in the cadences with their unusual diminished sevenths. The second half mounts upward in a forte
phrase and then takes up the opening refrain in a more
restless manner with a passing harmony in which B and
D naturals interpose between the chords of A flat and

the second inversion of its dominant seventh. If the conjecture that it was written in 1818 is correct it is the more wonderful for it contains in almost terse form so many elements of expression that we associate with the post-1821 period.

These six works are only included in this chapter because of size. They are very important compositions in which Schubert expresses in small compass the great range of his emotions, from the mere joy of music in no. 3 to the passion of no. 6. And apart from all this they form an important landmark in the history of music. Schubert's predecessors, either great or now forgotten, had written short piano works, but these are really the first masterpieces. Others were fugitive compositions, but these came to stay and must have greatly influenced both Schumann and Brahms. Mendelssohn went his own way with the *Lieder ohne Worte*, but Schubert had inaugurated a form much more free with possibilities of endless variation and extension. Although he carried over to his piano compositions the technique of his song writing he did not generally make them song-like for he clearly distinguished the difference between vocal and instrumental music, and although much of the latter is lyrical it is not metrical in the poetic sense.

E

VII

THE LARGER WORKS

WHAT has just been written about the *Moments Musicaux* applies equally to the Impromptus, opp. 90 and 142 except that, being bigger in form, they allowed for larger subjects and more development. They are all late works of 1827, and the first set of four was accepted by Haslinger who published the first two numbers in December of that year and himself bestowed the title of Impromptus. His firm did not issue the other two until 1857, and meanwhile another firm published the second set in 1838. Schubert had adopted Haslinger's title for these and had written it above the numbers 5-8. Hence op. 142 was known before op. 90 had been completed, and at a time when its first two numbers had probably been forgotten or at any rate become unavailable. Schumann in his famous article wrote that he could 'scarcely believe that Schubert really entitled these movements Impromptus. The first is evidently the first movement of a sonata, so perfectly carried out and concluded, that no doubt can exist about it'. His first doubt is refuted by Schubert himself but it would have been valid if applied to the first set. His second observation can be left for later consideration.

Op. 90 is at least as fine a set as the later one which has a weak spot in the variations, and it is remarkable that all eight numbers are in flat keys. The first, in C minor, is in serious vein and dramatic in those sections with a triplet pedal. The main subject consists of two four-bar sentences of exactly the same rhythmic pattern and very little difference in outline. The form is original, as the first sentence, after a long 'call' note, is a single solo line that is repeated with harmony. Then follows the second sentence, first unaccompanied and then accompanied. The whole sixteen bars are then repeated with unaltered melodic line but with more chromatic harmony so that the whole passage builds up to a fortissimo climax, and a series of cadential phrases wavering between C minor and A flat finally introduces a dominant seventh in favour of the latter key. A five-bar melody (Ex. 20, p. 44) follows, its iterated preliminary notes merely extending the three notes of the first melody, and the two are similar in many respects, like a winter and summer view of the same scene. The contours are similar but the warmth of the major key has added grace and colour to the curves. This charm grows as the theme merges into the key of C flat, and then back to A flat with a graceful turn. After the bass has taken up the melody this turn becomes prominent in a very delicate passage, and then, although the second subject endeavours to assert itself (at bar 82) the first enters in the bass and gradually becomes more powerful until, above a restless bass, it breaks into fragments and the chromatic bass forms harmonies which lead to the second subject in the bright key of G. There is still further development and although the first subject has the final word it fluctuates between minor and major almost to the end where it subsides peacefully in C major. Although the

C minor and A major melodies have been referred to as subjects their similarity is such that the work might be considered monothematic—like no. 3 in G flat. One might almost consider Schubert contemplating the bright and gloomy aspects of a situation as Robinson Crusoe did in his diary, for the absence of diverse subjects serves to maintain an objective unit round which thought and fancy may revolve.

No. 2 is full of nervous energy, as the phrasing of the first subject, analysed on p. 43, shows. The triplets running down a couple of octaves and then rising for a fresh descent maintain continuity, while the bass with its crotchet-minim figure maintains a further impulse. The second subject not only provides a vivid contrast with its key of B minor instead of the previous E flat, but also with fortissimo chords instead of pianissimo runs and with a 'springboard' rhythm (Ex. 45) that still retains, however, a similar bass and a vestige (though vital) of the triplet figure.

Ex. 45.

Later the figure of two minims lengthens to four with a semitone bend (Ex. 45a). The form of the work is a—b—a, but the coda is a development of b alternating between the two keys of B minor and E flat with aplomb, and concluding with a very brief reference to the triplet figure in a downward rush to the final chords.

The third number, written in G flat, was transposed to G by the publisher. It is a wonderfully sustained work of a hundred and seventy-two bars with long-drawn melodies and continuous sextuplet bass. Its interest is unflaggingly maintained by the varying contours of the upper line against the shifting harmonies which have been considered previously. There is some difficulty in deciding on the tempo of this work for Schubert wrote it in double alla breve time but the publisher altered it to alla breve. However, the indication Andante and the loving poise on the mediant shows that Schubert was in a contemplative, happy and unhurried mood.

No. 4, like 'Auf dem Wasser zu singen', commences in the key of A flat minor merely for the pleasure of bringing into relief the main tonic major key. What strikes one about this work, and others also, is its simplicity combined with originality. Anyone could write a series of descending arpeggios, turn them into an accompanying figure and put a melody below it! This is what Schubert has done for four pages and then repeated it *en bloc* after the Trio. The form is at first in regular two-bar phrases and each pair of arpeggios is divided by two bars of plain chords to form the series a—a—b—a—a in A flat minor. Then the series is repeated with the first a's in C flat (B major) and the last two in B minor, and yet there is no sense of monotony owing to the freshness and innocent audacity of the music. The chord passage is extended to eight bars

to lead back to A flat major and in each of three phrases
there is an emphatic iteration of three chords of dominant harmony in contrast to the tonic harmony of all the
arpeggios. Then after several bars of tonic harmony the
A flat arpeggios settle down on a tonic, subdominant and
dominant bass and there enters a lovely tenor melody in
four-bar phrases that break up into pairs as they mount
up in the treble clef.

It is a soaring melody rising in each bar until the
octave is attained:

Ex. 46.

It may be compared with another famous melody in an
opposite mood (Ex. 46a) with a falling fourth at the
beginning and end of its ineffectual effort to rise in the
middle. It is a transposed outline of the second subject
of the Unfinished Symphony, and the missing notes serve
only to emphasize that effort. If Schubert had not been
in tragic mood when writing the Symphony he would
have made this subject in G major rise triumphantly to
the major third, and the fact that it does not do so infuses
it with pathos. In the happy mood of this Impromptu
the superior notes in each bar are accented and so continue their course to a final climax in D flat. The return
to the home key brings in a variation of the melody in

even notes and then in its original version to end on a tonic seventh. This resolves, not in D flat, but in C sharp minor for the Trio.

The Trio opens quietly but after an upward leap to E a series of heavy suspensions and retardations with very few chords in their root positions produces agitation and unrest. Twice the melody mounts up to E above the stave and then subsides as the opening strain returns on the tonic major, but this is followed by an enlargement of the series of discords until the modulation back to the recapitulation of the Allegretto. The contrast between this and the Trio is very great in every respect. In melody, harmony and form they are so different, and the modulating links between the movements so short that one is amazed at the ease with which the mind is switched from one emotive response to the other without a sense of distortion or incongruity. There is great contrast in no. 2, but there the connecting modulations are less abrupt and more preparatory, whereas in no. 4 they are deceptive thus making the transitions (especially the first) more unexpected.

The second set of Impromptus opens up new vistas and it is difficult to understand why Schumann could have thought them to be connected with each other in any way. True, we may agree with him that the first and second have some agreement in character, but then we must also agree with him that the 'volatility' of the fourth is quite out of character, and he says the third is 'a set of indifferent or insignificant variations'. In fact his doubts are greater than his asservations and we can accept Schubert's own title in good faith.

Op. 142, no. 1 is based on two main subjects and is

divisible into two parts of almost exact length. The
opening is little more than a big preliminary flourish
of two similar six-bar phrases and the main subject commences at bar 13 with a figure (Ex. 47a) over a minimum
of bass.

Ex. 47.

It develops until its first two bars appear in the major in
octaves (b) and again develops until it settles in that key
after a big downward scale passage. Then it takes on the
melodic form of *c* and uses the whole melodic line of four
bars (a) compressed into three. When the left hand takes
the melody the right hand develops arpeggios that from
A flat major turn to the tonic minor for the next subject.
This is a Schubertian gem in which short phrases answer
one another above and below a continuous arpeggio
holding a central position. It modulates to C flat minor
and then to A flat major with two concluding bars to
return to the home key and an almost entire recapitulation from the beginning of the work, the only alterations
being in key relationships and a shortening of the A flat
minor subject. As the opening 'flourish' is repeated and
is used in the coda it must be called a subject but there

is no other reference to it. In the following analysis the first main subject is divided into three sections B, C and D, as it is so long.

	Bars	First Time	Second Time
A	1— 12	opening in F minor	130—141 slightly varied
B	13— 30	main subject in F minor	142—159 in F minor and major
C	30— 45	main subject in A flat	159—174 in F major
D	45— 67	melodic form of B.	174—196 in F major
E	68—129	3rd subject in A flat minor and major	197—239 in F minor and major
F	240—249	five bars of A in F minor and cadence bars.	

In regard to subjects this gives a form of a—b—c—a—b—c with no middle, and although it might be admitted into that vague class known as 'modified sonata' form, which has no development section, it is nothing like any Schubert 'first movement' form.

No. 2 is a favourite because of a gentle swinging rhythm and simple attractive melody which curves up to and down from the middle of the bar. The second phrase echoes the first four bars but with the thirds uppermost and then the eight bars are repeated an octave higher. A more imperative section follows with the fortissimo climax of Ex. 10, p. 24 leading to the opening melody with a subdued cadence phrase in which the bass glides in semitones from G flat to E flat. The Trio consists of a series of arpeggios above what is in several of these Impromptus a characteristic bass of crotchet and minim. Commencing in D flat (the sub-mediant of the first part) it gradually rises, starts again in D flat minor and passes through A major back to D flat for the recapitulation. The whole work is delight-ful in its contrasts and the middle passages in each sec-tion, in D flat and in A—both fortissimo—provide powerful climaxes.

No. 3 is a theme and variations. The theme itself is one of Schubert's happy peaceful rhythmic melodies associated with the 'Wiegenlied' (by Seidl), the Andante of the A minor Quartet and the second Entr'acte of *Rosamunde*. Although it opens in a manner similar to the Entr'acte it varies considerably after the first few notes. The theme is in two eight-bar sentences with a two-bar coda that is used attractively to close each variation but which cuts the work into sections. Hence there is not the continuity of movement that Schubert infused into the slow movement of the 'Wanderer' Fantasy or the A minor Sonata, and no tangible con-nection other than the use of the thematic outline.

The fact is that the melody is too characteristic for variation. It has such a definite mood of its own that it really seems inartistic to wrench it out of shape. It is curious that Schubert should have been so insensitive on such a point on other occasions also. One has only to think of his Variations on 'Trock'ne Blumen' and 'Sei mir gegrüsst' to see that this was so. Not only do these melodies mean much to us as definite songs but their very sound conveys the expression of the words and so makes them impossible for any other treatment. 'Die Forelle', used in the Quintet, has not the same kind of strong association, and 'Der Tod und das Mädchen' as used in the Quartet is only a series of solemn chords like those used in the Fantasy and so forms a perfect basis for variations, but the theme of this Impromptu falls between the two. Its mood is too definite and it is not thematic enough. The work is pleasant and certainly varied and some of the harmony is certainly Schubertian, but it is only a fine example of the many variations by minor composers on well-known songs.

The last number is highly original. It is a Fantaisie-Impromptu and like Chopin's work with that title it is in a large ternary form. Otherwise there is little similarity, for this is one of the few Schubert works in which there are no cantabile melodies. It is marked 'Allegro Scherzando' and it is truly 'volatile' although in the key of F minor. It begins with Ex. 48a and the first bar being repeated produces a variation of the poised opening mentioned on p. 40.

Ex.48.

But the D flats give it a nervous energy like a hawk on leash and it is not till the fourth bar that flight begins. Movement is more rapid when the cross-accents occur (Ex. 48b) and it mounts upward to a series of trills, and to still higher rapid ascents and descents. The airy flight of the following section in A flat also mounts and sinks in scale passages and then in an arpeggio figure (Ex. 49a) in alternating major and minor.

Ex. 49.

This soaring motion is continued almost to exhaustion as the mingled themes become short phrases between long pauses. The first subject returns to lead to a long development of bar 4 of Ex. 48a, and the coda makes the final triumphant ascent and a swift final rush down to rest.

The effect is one of great exhilaration and freedom of movement. The first page consists of the elements of Ex. 48a and b ending with trills and runs, and as this is repeated the dual pulsation is increased in length and power. The A flat section consists of very simple scale passages and one has to remember Gahy's remark on Schubert's pure rapid playing and his love of improvisation. The theme shown as 49a which emerges gains great power and closes on a dominant ninth before a silent pause bar. It then recommences in A to lead to great sweeping scale passages in A flat, returns and leads to alternating scales and the example last quoted. These very gradually fade away and the opening subject returns. Its last run, lengthened from seventeen notes in the bar to twenty-three, introduces Ex. 48a, bar 4, a figure which gradually forms chords that rise and fall in the right hand with a suppressed excitement fully realized in the coda. This is an eight-bar sentence thrice repeated, first in bare octaves (Ex. 49b), then with thirds and then with the single-bar rhythm of Ex. 49c, to end with a downward run of six octaves. It is a brilliant coda bringing resolution to the former impetuosity, and the outstanding character of the whole work is the manner in which the thematic fragments are worked up into great curves of sound.

In his last year Schubert wrote three more works of a similar nature but they were not published until 1868, under the title of *Drei Klavierstücke.* These are now more often referred to as Impromptus and it has been presumed that Schubert intended to produce another set of four as in op. 90 and 142. The three we have present certain problems and it is therefore only fair to presume also that Schubert would have thoroughly revised them before publication. The first two are very diffuse. In spite of the beauty of their parts there is a lack not only of continuity of thought but also of cohesion. Each presents a series of diverse pieces connected only by obvious modulating chords. No one could be more diverse on occasion than Schubert and we have no need to look further than the second and fourth numbers of op. 90 for obvious examples. But in each of these there are indefinable links that make us accept the contrasts as parts of a whole, like the obverse and reverse sides of a coin. This is not always so in the *Drei Klavierstücke* and if the composer wished to make these contrasts he should have bridged the gap or made the transition logical by means of a modulatory episode. That Schubert was aware of this problem is proved by his deletion of the Andantino in no.1, but it has been reinserted in various editions, and it is probable that he would have made other drastic alterations if he had lived to finish the set and prepare it for publication.

The first number is in a—b—a—c—a form and it is c that was deleted. The work opens with a vigorous movement in E flat minor in two-four time with a triplet bass that is at times taken up also by the treble and so produces in some phrases an alternating rhythm or a clash of rhythms. After the first double bar there are three rapid transitions from *p* to *ffz* as the triplets lead to the chords of G flat, A flat and E flat respectively, and a few bars later the same series have a decrescendo in splendid contrast. The subject is repeated in the tonic major but after sixteen bars it is altered until full chords with cross-rhythms add further impetus. A casual modulation brings in a new subject in B. It is an Andante in rhapsodic form with a passionate middle section and contrasts well with the previous subject which also follows it. Here is an excellent ternary composition, but it was followed by a pastoral 'andantino' and a recapitulation of the first 'Allegro assai', and both these should be omitted and so leave a very satisfactory work.

The next number as it stands is in rather worse case. It also is in a—b—a—c—a form with c itself in a—b—a form. The opening Allegretto is a guileless six-eight melody in E flat with a lovely poise in the seventh bar that prolongs the first section into a nine-bar sentence. The rest is in four-bar phrases. This little 'pastorale' is followed by a stormy movement in which pianissimo phrases in six-eight time are divided by bars of three-four with sforzando emphasis, and this gives way to the return of the first subject. Here again we have a complete and coherent work, but a tonic seventh follows to lead to a new subject in A flat minor in alla breve time. It is a beautiful melody, first in two five-bar phrases and then unbroken for sixteen bars. The key, after a Neapolitan sixth, alternates between A flat minor and C flat and closes in the latter key. This becomes enharmonically B, but minor, for a fresh subject, an impressive melody of unusual rhythm in eighteen bars, which modulates back for the A flat minor repeat. This section itself would form an admirable *Moment Musical* but its closing chords are continued to form a modulation to E flat and a return of the first subject.

The last number is concise in ternary form. The first subject in C is syncopated and quickly modulates with little arpeggios here and there, from which a fresh subject soon evolves. This passes through various keys to a sharp close in the tonic. After a bar's rest there is a skeleton modulation to D flat for the next subject. This is a dance measure in three-two time with a rhythm of two minims and two crotchets in each bar, the melody being first in the treble and then in the tenor. This also passes through various keys while the basic rhythm is maintained throughout by the bass. This rhythm then merges into that of the first subject which returns in the home key and concludes with a vigorous coda.

Compared with the Impromptus these three works are rather thin in texture and less emotional, but their very simplicity and masterly technique (apart from general form) seem to indicate that Schubert was breaking new ground, and once he had come to a decision on the formal structure would have produced works in a 'free fantasia' form. He had gone a long way to this end years before when he composed op. 15 and it was called a Fantasy, but because it has a superficial resemblance to the sonata form we are apt to overlook its real structure.

The Fantasy was composed in November 1822 while Schubert was scoring the Unfinished Symphony, a task which he began on October 30th. It was published as a *Fantaisie pour le Pianoforte* and not until fifty years later did it receive its present title. This was quickly accepted and made the foundation of the theory that Schubert had indeed written a set of variations on his song 'Der Wanderer', and made it the basis of the whole work. This theory was challenged in 1951[1] and is well worth reconsideration. In the first place it is not the song that is taken but merely eight bars out of a total of seventy-two, and secondly this quotation is not a 'literal' one for the melodic line has been altered. It was composed in 1816 and became very popular, but when the Fantasy appeared no one remarked on the similarity between the two themes. This was due to its brevity and its alterations, but chiefly to its comparative insignificance in the song. What must have been much more important then were the first and last parts of the song and only our knowledge of the variations has given us a deeper understanding of those phrases quoted in the Fantasy.

In 1817 Schubert composed the song 'Der Jüngling und der Tod' which commences 'Die Sonne sinkt' (cf. the phrase in 'Der Wanderer'—'Die Sonne dunkt'), and although the voice part is different the prelude may be

---

[1] Maurice Brown, *Schubert's Variations*, p. 49.

compared with the first part of the Fantasy theme in
Ex. 50.

Ex. 50.

It seems evident that the phrase with its reiterated
dominant and the cadence with rising treble (an inner
part in *a*) and falling bass had a deep significance for
Schubert and remained with him for years;[1] but to sup-
pose that he recollected the song, considered a few bars
of it suitable for variation and then wrote the whole
work round it is too presumptuous. It is much more
likely that he started the work at the beginning with the
first movement in mind, and then, with the idea of main-
taining the dactyl rhythm for each movement, the
Adagio theme rose almost unbidden to his mind.

This is a more massive Fantasy than any of those previously written, for they consisted generally of comparatively short sections. This, however, follows the sonata in

[1] See E. G. Porter, *Schubert's Song Technique* for other
examples.

its layout, the movements being free in form, running
from one to the other without a break, and linked by the
similarity of the main themes. It was in essence the pre-
cursor of the new music forms and cyclic symphonies and
symphonic poems of a later period. Its vital statistics are
188, 56, 353 and 123 bars. The shortness of the Adagio is
counterbalanced by the length of its bars, some of which
take up the whole width of the page and others even
double that space. The Presto is in three-four time but
much of it is really six-four or even twelve-four rhythm
(which would about halve its actual bar length), and
being in scherzo and trio form the repeat of the first part
has to be counted as it is altered considerably.

The whole work is an expression of power and tenderness, but much more purposeful and forceful than the
'Unfinished' as though Schubert were asserting his unconquerable spirit. Here he is not submerged by fate or
trying to rise above it but facing it with determination.
The first full solid chords with their third uppermost and
the big upward following swing announce this spirit.
They are two characteristics of Schubertian confidence
and aspiration, and this force takes fresh wing after a
chromatic run in the bass for a first trial of a new key
(at the first pause). But the main subject enters again
and gradually builds up to a powerful diminished seventh
and then subsides as though to lead to the key of the
dominant. However, the previous dissonance crashes in
again as though to deny this modulation, but this in turn
follows the same sequence which falters, by syncopation,
in its cadence and the melody rises to the mediant of
the G major chord and again hesitates before deciding
to slide tenderly on to the mediant of E major for a new

subject. This is similar to the opening (Ex. 51a) in rhythm but has an entirely different character and much more evolutionary power because of the notes in the second bar (Ex. 51b).

Ex. 51.

a (bar 1)   b (bar 47)

c (bar 112)   etc.

It passes through various phases until the first subject reappears (at bar 70) and then takes on more of its partner's vigour as it develops above or below swift runs or arpeggios. Even when this forceful passage concludes it still holds sway but (Ex. 51c) with sweetly (dolce) lengthened phrases for many bars until the two subjects seem to join force in a grand peroration that is followed by a passage based merely on the dactyl rhythm with pulsating stresses as though undecided whether to speak forcefully or tenderly, and finally decides on the latter for the Adagio.

This set of variations is a movement without breaks, swinging between the heights and depths of emotion. The theme is really only four bars long, being repeated with an altered cadence to lead to the relative major for a brighter but more nervous expression followed by ominous tremolos low in the bass. Then follows a more energetic section, the excitement of which decreases to lead to the tonic major. Here the melody enters with a serene air but soon alternates between major and minor,

settling down in the latter with the melody in an inner
part and leading to a tumultuous series of rising and
descending passages—the first through three and a half
octaves. These then become big chords to lead to the final
variation in which the melody is above a swiftly moving
bass as though riding above a subsiding tempest. The
form is much more free than Schubert's other variations,
and because the theme is for practical purposes a four-
bar phrase the whole of the middle section of the movement is in reality a set of very short variations that
produce great diversity, compared for instance with
those of op. 42.

The Presto (or Scherzo) is based on three figures.
The first (Ex. 52, bar 1) derives from the bass at the
end of the Adagio, the second (Ex. 52, bar 2) from the
basic opening theme of the work, and the third (Ex. 52,
bar 5) from the 'cadence' of the fourth bar of the basic
theme.

Ex. 52.

These elements assume all sorts of arrangements and by
the absence of any true cadence carry on for thirty bars
to a pause and then on again for another twenty-eight
bars to a big climax. The second bar then takes on a
four-bar rhythm in a lilting melody followed by an up-
stepping bass in the same rhythm. These 'subjects' then
alternate to lead to the peaceful and contemplative Trio
which is in two-bar rhythm, and so back to a résumé of
the Scherzo and the climax noted in Ex. 9, p. 23. The

Allegro starts off in fine fugal style with the basic theme extended to eight bars as the subject. After the fourth entry of the subject there is a powerful development, based largely on the big drop in bars 5 and 6 of the subject, in various rhythms and above or below flying arpeggios and working up to a massive climax and coda.

THE DUETS

To these may be added Schubert's own arrangements for duet of his two Overtures in Italian Style (D.592, 597) and the overtures to *Alfonso* (op. 69) and *Fierabras* (D.798). The arrangement of the last named, published in 1827 as op. 76, was made by Czerny. These bring the total to thirty-five works or sixty individual compositions and the fact that all were finished is an indication of Schubert's keen interest in this form of writing. There are various reasons for this, one being that his friends delighted in works that, with their aid, could be performed immediately on completion; for several of them, especially Josef von Gahy, were able to partner him at the piano. It also accounts for the fact that they are generally light in character with brilliance rather than depth. There was also a market for such works and seventeen of them were published in Schubert's lifetime, this total not including the overture arrangements.

Although publication was very useful at the time it was probably also unfortunate as it gave the public a mistaken view of Schubert's stature, suggesting that he was a minor composer of dances, songs and duets. Nevertheless, the list is an imposing one ranging from the slightest works to the important fantasies, divertissements and the great Sonata in C; and examination of these will go to show that Schubert enjoyed writing duets because they provided by the use of four hands the whole keyboard for the exercise of his contrapuntal skill. The themes, subjects and accompanying figures exchange parts with wonderful skill and effect, and the use of melody and counter-melody occur with great freedom and provide much pleasure to both performers.

The duet developed as the pianoforte increased its compass and volume, and as it became an integral part of domestic music-making. There are a few early works for this medium by the Englishman Theodore Smith but the first important compositions were Mozart's sonatas, and although Beethoven wrote four works they are of minor interest. Hence Schubert made a valuable contribution at a time when this form of composition was practically in its infancy and showed what really could be done, for he thoroughly explored the new field that Mozart had discovered. His works are of interest to both performer and listener. Themes may appear in either part and rarely does the bass have a dull line of mere accompaniment, for even simple chords are brightened by passing notes or rhythmic figures. The treble is naturally more florid at times for such passages are more telling in the upper register, and it more generally has the main subjects in order to give them prominence, but apart from these considerations the bass player often has the main interest.

With a few exceptions the works are gay and light-hearted, evidently written with pleasure in order to give pleasure. Schubert did not unburden his mind here as he did in the larger solo works, but he provided plenty of interest in his own inimitable manner. Some of the Dances are very short. The four Polonaises of 1818 are very varied but nearly all in eight- or sixteen-bar sections. The first is in D minor with some delightful modulations and the fourth commences with Ex. 53, carried on in the next section to D flat with Ex. 53a, then on to A flat and back again to F.

Ex. 53.

The Polonaise sections are generally rather florid and the Trios melodic. In the set of 1825 the form is lengthened. The first has a two bar introduction for both parts so that the form is 2 + 8 + 12 and 2 + 8 + 16. The third has twelve and twenty-four bars in each part and the fourth has 12 + 28 and 12 + 20, and this extension allows for more variation in the internal rhythm of the phrasing.

The Fugue is an unimportant work. It was composed while Schubert was at Baden with friends. He and Lachner, who often played duets together, had a friendly competition in writing a fugue, and they played this op. 152 on the abbey organ the day after its composition. The Allegro and Andante of 1813 are very simple movements and may have been intended for a sonata. The treble part is nearly all in octaves which suggests that the work may have been written at a later date for teaching purposes.

All the Marches have Trios and rely for their attractiveness on a rich vein of melody, on figured accompaniments with vigorous rhythm, and on rich harmonies and striking modulations. The first of the Heroic Marches is short and simple with a stately stepping bass and a quiet trio. The other two are more elaborate, the marches being complex pieces of workmanship of great vigour, to which the trios form melodious contrasts. The opening of no. 2 (Ex. 54a) gives an idea of what is to be expected.

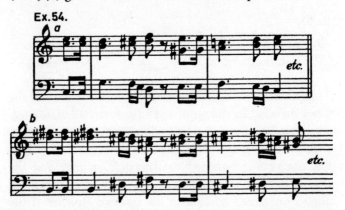

Ex. 54.

The bass maintains the key of C while the treble colours it in contrary motion (both parts are in octaves). The march then passes through the keys of A and F and then the bass ascends chromatically to B natural for the repeat. The second half proceeds with reversed motion as at Ex. 54b in the key of B and at last closes triumphantly in C. Then the bass rises gradually to E flat as the dominant of the Trio which is a flowing melody in thirds. No. 3 commences in somewhat the same way but becomes very melodious and the second half is in the flat sub-dominant for a pianissimo passage. In the Trio the treble part has some delightful phrases in canon.

It is not possible to go into detail in all these works, and it should not be necessary, for their charm is self-evident. It is, indeed, surprising that most of them are not as popular as the first of the three Military Marches.

This work in D owes its fame to the gaiety of its march and the romantic air of its trio. The bass has a solo introduction like a trumpet call. The trio is in the subdominant and passes through G minor to B flat, much of its charm being due to its poised rhythm, for most of the four-bar phrases commence with four notes on the dominant so that each starts as a straight line ending in a curve or turn to the cadence. The second march is shorter, and the third, which is the longest, has been unduly neglected. It has a bold and vigorous melody in E flat answered by quieter strains in C flat, but the bass of the trio is rather monotonous for the player although it sounds quite attractive below the melody.

It would be difficult to choose the best of the Six Marches (op. 40) for they all have special points of interest. The trio of the first has a lovely broad flowing melody; the second opens with alternate calls between the players in a very entertaining manner, and they do not really unite forces until the trio enters. The third is full of sforzando surprises and, like the previous march, has a suave Trio in perfect contrast. The fourth opens with trumpet calls interspersed with melodic phrases in triplets, 'maestoso', and its Trio is like a chorale enlivened by a tripping bass. The last of the set is 'con brio' with some startling modulations but less general variety than the others.

No. 5 is quite different. It is an Andante movement in E flat minor and the solemn majesty of its themes should have made it a general favourite. It is worthy of a place beside the funeral marches of Beethoven and Chopin although it has no desolate gloom or bitterness. The pain is there in the sforzando discords, and the

sorrow swells to tears as the first big crescendo turns
pathetically to a close after a big falling phrase:

Ex. 55.

The key changes to F sharp minor and the bass enlarges
the phrase of the above example by turning the rising
fifths to sixths and sevenths, and when they are taken
up by the treble in A major the effect is still more
pathetic. Another big crescendo brings the return of the
more gloomy opening subject after which the Trio affords
relief with a tender strain in the tonic major, but after
twelve bars the melody ceases and reiterated chords
gather force only to die away in a dominant cadence. This
marvellous little emotional climax is effected by changing
the chord of B flat to G major and back again in the
course of four bars with a rhythm entirely different from
that of the rest of the Trio. There is a similar passage
later but as there has been a modulation to C flat it is
not deceptive like the above but leads back to the original
key and melody.

The two *Characteristic Marches* are 'allegro vivace' and both commence with a series of drum beats, the first on tonic and dominant and the second on the tonic. The first sets the rhythm for the whole work with two tonic and one dominant quavers to the beat. The notes vary of course as the work proceeds, sometimes taking other parts of a chord or descending the scale, but always with the 2—1—2—1 bar-rhythm which the treble generally follows. Sentences swing into one another with varying modulations and accents in irresistible rhythms which are carried over into a tuneful trio. The second march is naturally somewhat similar in character but the treble has a different bar-rhythm and modulates more abruptly and further afield. The trio has an arpeggio bass and the march on repetition has a brilliant coda of thirty-two bars as the bass descends in C first to low G and then to A flat with a rising treble fortissimo. This big crescendo is repeated with varied bass to B flat and by a series of transitions to the final cadence. It is surprising that these vigorous works have not been arranged for military band for they are certainly 'characteristic'.

The *Grand Funeral March* was composed on 'the occasion of the death of Alexander I, Emperor of all the Russias'. It is a pompous lament in C minor suitable for a state occasion but it may be suspected that Schubert was not deeply moved either by sympathy or inspiration. Nevertheless it is a fine piece of music *per se* with all the suitable minor thirds, diminished sevenths, drum-rolls, and clashing cymbals. There are the emotional crescendos, two of them to triple forte with a sudden fall, and the heavy stepping bass. The Trio is in A flat, its lighter quality being subdued by a drumming bass that rumbles unceasingly in a part monotonous for the player. The Heroic March, composed a little later for the Coronation of Nicholas I, is also a show piece of imposing substance —March, Trio, March II, Trio II, March I and Coda. After a four-bar fanfare the march proceeds with plenty of variety in both parts. It is in A minor with a Trio in E minor which has an attractive but not stately rhythm (Ex. 56a).

The second march is 'allegro giusto' with a splendid bass, again in A minor, below alternate *ff* and *p* phrases into which there soon enters the rhythm of Ex. 56b. The second Trio is in F with the main cadences in D minor. The Coda consists mainly of material from the first Trio and March.

The *Kindermarsch* is a little souvenir of Schubert's happy time at Graz in 1827 when Madame Pachler persuaded him to compose a little duet for herself and her son Faust, then seven years old. He wrote, 'I'm afraid it will not meet with your approval as I don't feel myself well qualified for writing things in this style'. It is short and simple but with some modulatory phrases that might be awkward for a child, and the Trio has three notes against two.

Some of the variations are very fine works, the two

sets on original themes being especially beautiful. In
these Schubert was not satisfied with mere skeletons of
tunes but wrote charming little subjects that are themselves masterpieces in miniature. Op. 82, no. 2 was not
published until 1860 and is entirely unconnected with
op. 82 which was published in 1827. It has a march-like
introduction closing with a cadenza, and the following
theme is in two eight-bar sentences, bars 13 and 15 being
the same as bars 1 and 3 and only altered at the end to
form a final cadence. This is opposite to the usual method
of commencing two sentences in a similar manner and
varying the latter halves, and adds more excitement to
the middle of the theme which has some attractive part
writing and naturally gives rise to four pleasant variations concluding on a bass 'andante' of two bars. In it
there is one of Schubert's deceptive 'modulations'—
from B flat to B flat—and then follows a little cadenza in
the treble, and the time changes from duple to triple for
a brilliant little finale.

Op. 35 is a much bigger work, there being seven
variations on a twenty-four-bar theme. The melody
commences in A flat but is coloured by passing chords
over a sequential bass (Ex. 57a), and the middle sentence
has a delightful canon outlined in Ex. 57b.

Ex. 57.

The last sentence, although somewhat like the first, modulates to B flat minor and passes to a cadence in C major just before the final phrase in the home key. The variations are very interesting for both performers. In the first the bass has two melodic lines below the theme much varied in triplet rhythm, in the second it has long running passages and commences the canon of the second sentence before the entry of the treble. As there is so much harmonic variety in the theme itself there is little need for a change of key and it is not until variation 5 that the signature is altered to A flat minor in which key there is a very beautiful change to A major and back again. The 'più lento' of number 6 is a simple but most impressive variation, both part-writing and harmony being very beautiful. The last variation is in twelve-eight time and not only extends the theme but adds to it, for the little figure in canon is so changed as to be practically a new melody. Three times the harmony changes quickly from A flat to A and back again with amazing effect, and the work concludes with scale passages that cover almost the whole of the keyboard.

The other sets of variations suffer to some extent because they are based on French themes[1] in an idiom evidently not congenial to Schubert. There is no warmth in them and he could infuse very little into the variations. They are intellectual but hardly inspired, and indeed the same may be said of most of the Mozart and Beethoven sets on other composers' themes. They all did much better with their own original themes as found in the sonatas and other works.

[1] Some of the themes have not been traced. These may be by Schubert himself but even so they have not served his purpose well.

The first of the sets on a French song is op. 10, and was dedicated to Beethoven 'by his admirer and worshipper F. Schubert'. It consists of seven straightforward variations on a sixteen-bar melody, with a concluding Tempo di Marcia of a hundred and twelve bars in fantasia style. Here the theme is broken up and stated in various parts, where quotations from the countersubjects of the previous sections also appear. In the first two variations the key of E minor is retained but no. 3 is in C which modulates to E flat in the first part with a powerful return in the second half. No. 5 is in the tonic major and the melody is reshaped and becomes recognizably Schubertian. The key of E minor then returns for a 'più lento' that works up to an exciting climax for the entry of the Finale in E major.

The op. 82 Variations on a theme from Hérold's opera *Marie* were composed soon after a performance of that work in Vienna. As the theme itself is a mere skeleton it would need a Beethoven to discourse on it with logic and persuasive interest. This was not really Schubert's sphere, but this is not to deny that the work is of interest. The last variation, like that of op. 10, is a long fantasia.

Another set of variations was published as op. 84, no. 1, *Andantino varié, composé sur des motifs originaux français*, but the Andantino is the one and only theme for this short composition. Op. 84, no. 2 is known as a *Rondeau brillant*, and both works were abstracted from op. 63, no. 1 of which was published as a *Divertissement en forme d'une marche brillante et raisonné composé sur des motifs originaux français*. Hence they form together one three-movement work. The *Divertissement*,

F

though in 'March' form, is a finely-worked-out sonata movement. This should be followed by the Andantino and the Rondeau, and as all the French tunes employed were probably popular at the time, the complete work would have been accepted as an expert and ingeniously arranged pot-pourri.

The *Divertissement à la hongroise*, op. 54, includes Hungarian melodies much more congenial to Schubert. The opening, without the snap of the grace notes, is a favourite Schubert phrase form with the main movement in the middle:

Ex. 58.

It is similar to Ex. 53, p. 139. It is immediately developed extensively in both parts with dazzling key changes, dynamics and varied figuration. A short simple march in regular rhythm allows a brief respite and another theme enters (Ex. 58b), the first two notes being like the crack of a whip as the phrases rise in pitch and force to the full octave (*c*). Tempo and stress continually vary and the sudden *sff* beats are most effective. Other rhythmic subjects enter and the whole work is interesting and exciting for both players, with a touch of frenzy or pathos here and there in presumed Hungarian style.

The Fantasy, op. 103 in F minor commences somewhat in the strain of the above work but maintains a calm rhythm until the bass introduces a broader descending counter-melody in A flat and a little later a bold rising marcato subject. This and the first subject alternate to a close in F, which is sharpened to introduce a very powerful Largo. The following Allegro vivace is one of Schubert's finest scherzos, with some brilliant counterpoint and flashing key changes. It is in A, and a short Trio in D is marked 'con delicatezza' but has a middle section starting in F sharp and working up in six bars to double forte on some clashing chords, the last being a diminished fifth on the notes D flat, E and G. After four beats' silence the opening phrase of the Trio enters very softly in the unexpected key of C and gradually works to a return to the Scherzo. The last few notes of this are altered to rise to C sharp which becomes the chord of D flat to herald the return of the main subject in F minor which works up in fugal style to a most powerful conclusion.

The other Fantasies are early works. The third, in C minor, was called *Grande Sonate* and is a fine work full of romantic originality despite its Mozartian similarities. The introductory Adagio of four bars announces the chief theme of the work—a falling chromatic phrase that dominates the whole work with great ingenuity. It becomes the subject of the first movement, which commences as a fugue in four parts, and is then developed for three pages without a break. There is no second subject, but its place is taken by a more lyrical form of the motto theme in the relative major. A re-statement of the subject leads to an Andante amoroso and then to an

Allegro based on a variant of the subject. An Adagio of great dramatic power follows and the work concludes with a Fugue on the original subject.

Of the Overtures the two most interesting are those in F and D. The first has an impressive Adagio with a key signature of four flats but is more in D flat and C major rather than in the more orthodox key of F minor. The following Allegro opens pompously but has a delicate lyrical second subject and a vivacious six-eight finale. The work in D, although an arrangement of an orchestral overture in 'Italian' style, makes a fine duet. This also has an Adagio introduction and after eight bars there enters the lovely melody which Schubert used later in the E flat overture known as *Rosamunde*. There it is enlarged and has a more impressive prelude. In this version in D the melodic line is slightly different; there is not the same dramatic tensity and it dies away gradually to a *ppp*. Here also the Finale is in six-eight time, marked Vivace, and this section was also enlarged to form the conclusion of the *Rosamunde* overture. Deutsch states that it is doubtful whether Schubert himself gave this work the sub-title *in italienischen Stile*, but here, as in the other overture (D597), it is justified to some extent by the use of a 'guitar' accompaniment to the main melodies with a Rossini flavour.

The Sonata in B flat, op. 30, was composed in 1818, a year of many duets. It is a rather short concise work in three movements and interesting throughout. Like several other happy works it commences with a sort of trial flourish to set the key and mood. The first subject is an eight-bar melody with a counter-subject in the bass, and quickly arrives at the second subject in D flat. This is a melodic two-bar phrase that is repeated three times below a running treble which continues to weave itself into a delightful variation of the subject. The development is based first on a short figure of a rising third that occurred in the transition section, and then takes the running figures through a series of modulations. In the reprise the first subject is in the home key but the second is in G flat, and returns to B flat by way of B minor, E, A minor and D minor.

The second movement is 'Andante con moto', commencing in D minor—a melodious subject in four-part writing. The treble then takes up fragments of the subject and a march-like section leads to the reprise of the first subject in the tonic major. Thus the movement ends in D major and the following Allegretto opens in B flat, this major third shift being one of Schubert's means of expressing happiness. This movement is in an easy-going six-eight time in sonata form, with its second subject in G flat (in C flat in the reprise). The development section supplies contrast by taking a bass figure from the codetta, emphasizing it, and then turning it into big scale passages in the bass. The whole is in light-hearted mood and recalls the good humour of some of Haydn's sonatas.

The Rondo in D, op. 138, although written in the same year, was not published until seventeen years later, and then under the spurious sub-title *Notre amitié est invariable*. This was for long supposed to refer to the friendly crossing of hands by the players in the coda, but it was discovered that this was due only to a rearrangement of the parts by the publisher who also omitted a complete section of the work.[1]

[1] Maurice Brown, *Schubert, A Critical Biography*, p. 81.

It commences with a lilting melody in polonaise rhythm, its initial arpeggio ending on an appoggiatura making it easily recognizable on each return, and the turn in the second bar is used later for various modulations, and as a bridge passage to the next subject in F, D minor and B flat. It is a pleasant, tuneful work, its main key contrast being between the D major of the first subject and the F major of the second.

The other Rondo, op. 107, was written ten years later. It is a beautiful work in clarity of form and perfection of expression. Its opening is a gem in two-part writing, with its phrasing, dynamics, and final turn in the treble above a smooth flowing bass:

Ex.59.

This turn, as in the previous Rondo, is a motif that is frequently used and occurs over thirty times in the course of the work. The first subject itself is in ternary form, as the first sentence is repeated to lead to an eight-bar sentence in the dominant, also repeated, and leading back to the first sentence again. The second subject is nominally in the dominant but the major triads of B and C sharp occur frequently and form richly coloured passages. An episode in C major is bold with strong modulations, and the return of the main subjects full of pleasant surprises. The second subject appears in the tenor, first in F and then in B flat below a vibrating treble in triplets, and the final appearance of the first subject is also in the tenor, in the home key, below running treble passages which are a sheer delight in a work that is wholly satisfying to performers and listeners alike.

The Sonata in C, published as a 'Grand Duo' op. 140, was composed in 1824 at about the same time as the splendid variations in A flat. It is a very big work that has been much discussed for its size, power and 'orchestral' style. It was Schumann who first suggested that it was really an arrangement of a symphony and so, in a way, belittled the work as a duet, and Tovey wrote in the same strain; indeed three attempts have been made to score it for full orchestra. There is, however, little technique in this duet that is not to be found in the others. The varied effects of triplet ornamentation high in the treble and the sustained notes occur in other duets. Sustained octaves, to which Tovey takes special objection, are prominent in some of the solo works, as pointed out elsewhere. The longest notes in the Finale of this work are not meant to be sustained audibly as they would be by an orchestral instrument. They are held so that they will sound as overtones to the bass, as Ex. 60 shows.[1]

[1]The reader will note this effect if he depresses the G sharp (without sounding it), and then strikes the bottom E *staccato*. That will cause the high note to vibrate.

Ex. 60.

The chief difficulties in discussing the work are that it is somewhat outside the Schubert 'idiom', and that the modern piano is too heavy to allow the various effects to come through as Schubert intended. He himself was well pleased with it and mentioned it twice as a 'sonata' in his letters (to Ferdinand in July and to Schwind in August of 1824), and played it with Gahy in 1827.

It has been orchestrated by Joachim, Antony Collins and Karl Salomon but their efforts have not been very successful, and the fact that they had to alter Schubert should prove that he was writing for the piano. Joachim changed the tempo of the last movement, and the programme note to Collins's arrangement stated that the figuration in the last movement is keyboard music, and 'not even an orchestra of Heifetzes would feel at home with it'. Also the second theme in the first movement had to have 'improvised' support, and the following triplets gave difficulty. Joachim divided them between violins and flutes to avoid this, but Collins 'risked' the violins alone.

It is a work of imposing size and character. Its opening subject is very significant, its first phrase being based on major and minor thirds like that of the great C major Symphony.

Ex. 61.

The whole subject consists of four phrases, *a* and *c* being in bare octaves and *b* and *d* harmonized in D minor and C major respectively. Hence it is similar in structure to the solo Sonata, op. 42, composed a year later. After a few bars the bass takes up the subject with *a* and *c* fortissimo and *b* and *d* piano. The modulating episode is brief but involved and leads to A flat in which key the second subject is announced in the tenor. It is a nine-bar sentence and its opening:

Ex. 62. ·

is so closely allied to the first subject that in later development their phrases often take on each other's characteristics. The whole movement is a closely woven fabric of themes and counter-themes that is well worth bar by bar analysis, and the conflict between major and minor, fortissimo and pianissimo is highly dramatic. The minor fall in Ex. 61a plays an important part, as does the rising sixth that commences Ex. 62, and in the final bars the rising phrase (Ex. 61b) passes through a pathetic transformation before the close in C major.

The conflict in this movement is well controlled by its 'allegro moderato' tempo and by the broad curves of the main subjects, but in the other movements (except the Trio) there is not this amalgamation of speed and breadth, and this is what takes the work as a whole outside Schubert's usual method of expression. The second movement is an Andante in three-eight, and the last movement in two-four time. The various subjects naturally have their own rhythm and individual form but the accompanying parts nearly always maintain a semiquaver movement that creates an intense continuity but avoids definite contrast.

The Andante immediately establishes this close texture in beautiful four-part writing. This continues for twenty-five bars, after which there is a brief modulation to E major for a marcato subject that in due course gives place to a long passage in A flat. This is built largely on a short phrase with a turn that dominates the whole section, and which has been noted as resembling the slow movement of Beethoven's Second Symphony. The Scherzo is stark, almost fierce at times, and there is no contrasting melodic section usual to this form with Schubert. Hence the Trio, with its big phrases in dotted minims over a slow-moving bass, produces an air of mystery and a terrific contrast to the Trio. The finale is very long, energetic and almost breathless in its impetuosity, forming a fitting conclusion to a really great work.

The Allegro, op. 144 is another work issued under a publisher's sub-title *Lebensstürme* ('Life's tempests') which, as is usual in such cases, is quite misleading. The work is in A minor and has many strenuous passages contrasting with tender and pathetic strains, but it has not the deep significance of the symphony or quintet composed in the same year. Nevertheless it is a splendid work in sonata form running to over 600 bars. But the form is very free for the constant recurrence of the main subjects gives it the aspect of a Rondo.

The first subject is in two parts, a bold sort of fanfare or challenge of ten bars and a pleading response of twelve bars (Ex. 63a).

Ex. 63.

The bass then takes up the latter theme below the same
tenor accompaniment with answering phrases in canon
in the alto, and a climax is reached with big chords of
the Neapolitan sixth. Modulation then proceeds until
the bass with the rhythm of the next example descends
to form the bass of the second subject in A flat (Ex. 63b).
All this is worked out with much variety of part writing
and modulation.

Two brief quotations will give some idea of the bold-
ness of the harmony in Schubert's last year.

Ex. 64.

Ex. 64a commences from the Neapolitan sixth mentioned
above, and this is followed by a sequence a tone lower.
Ex. 64b is from the codetta in which the bass refers to
the first subject; it is slightly altered in the reprise and
used again with stronger discords a little later. The work
is well worth study, for it is a fine example of the flexi-
bility Schubert could attain in a first-movement form.

APPENDICES

LIST OF SCHUBERT'S WORKS FOR PIANO

Title	Opus No.	Date composed	Dedication
7 Variations, F major		? 1810	
42 'Menuette'		1812-18	
'Andante', C major		1812	
'Menuette'.		1813-16	
Sonata, E major		1815	
Sonata, C major (3 movements only)		1815	
10 Variations		1815	
2 Waltzes		1815	
'Adagio', G major		1815	
'Walzer, Ländler und Ecossaisen'	18	c. 1815-21	
'Ecossaisen'		1815-25	
54 'Deutsche'		1815-27	
66 'Ecossaises'		1815-24	
20 Waltzes	127	1815-24	
'Deutsche'		1815-24	
6 'Walzer'		1815-23	

Title	Opus No.	Date composed	Dedication
Sonata, E major (published as 5 'Klavierstücke')		1816	
'Erste Walzer',	9	c. 1816-21	
7¹ 'Ländler'		1816-24	
Adagio and Rondo, E major¹	145	1817	
2 Scherzos		1817	
Sonata, A minor	164	1817	
Sonata, E minor		1817	
Sonata, E Flat major (original D Flat major)	122	1817	
Sonata, F Sharp minor (unfinished)		1817	
Sonata, B major	147	1817	
Sonata, A Flat major		1817	
Variations on a Theme by Anselm Hüttenbrenner		? 1817	
Scherzo, D major		1818	
'Adagio', E major		1818	
March, E major		1818	
Sonata, C major (unfinished)		1818	
Sonata, F minor (unfinished)		1818	
'Klavierstück', A major		? 1818	
Sonata, C Sharp minor (unfinished)		1819	

¹ The Rondo is the finale of the Sonata in E minor; the Adagio is the slow movement of the Sonata in F minor.

Title	Opus No.	Date composed	Dedication
Sonata, A major	120	1819	
Variation on a Theme by Diabelli[2]		1821	
Fantasy, C major ("Wanderer")	15	1822	Emanuel Karl, Edler von Liebenberg
Sonata, A minor	143	1823	
12 'Ländler'	171	1823	
6 'Moments musicaux'[3]	94	c. 1823-27	
'Deutsche und Ecossaisen'	33	before 1824	
'Deutsche'		1824 (publ. 1931)	
'Albumblatt', G major		1825	Anna Hönig
Sonata, C major (unfinished, "Reliquie")		1825	
Sonata, A minor	42	1825	Archduke Rudolph
Sonata, D major	53	1825	Karl Maria von Bocklet

[2] This was No. 38 of 50 variations by 50 different composers on a Waltz supplied by Diabelli. Beethoven used this for his famous 'Diabelli' variations.
[3] Originally 'musicals'.

Title	Opus No.	Date composed	Dedication
'Damenländler und Ecossaisen'	67	1825	
'Valses sentimentales'	50	1826	"Hommage aux belles Viennoises"
Sonata, G major (published as 'Fantaisie, Andante, Menuet et Allegretto')	78	1826	Josef, Edler von Spaun
'Grazer Galopp'		1827	
12 'Grazer Walzer'	91	1827	
4 'Impromptus'	142	1827	
'Valses nobles'	77	1827	
'Allegretto', C minor		1827	Ferdinand Walcher
4 'Impromptus'	90	1827	
3 'Klavierstücke'		1828	
Sonata, C minor		1828	Johann Nepomuk Hummel[1]

[1] Schubert's dedication. These three sonatas actually appeared with the publisher's dedication to Robert Schumann.

Title	Opus No.	Date composed	Dedication
Sonata, A major		1828	Hummel
Sonata, B Flat major		1828	Hummel
Sonata, E minor (unfinished)		?	

DUETS

Title	Opus No.	Date composed	Dedication
3 Fantasies			
Overture, C major ("Italian style") (arr. Composer)		1810-13	
Overture, D major ("Italian style") (arr. Composer)		1817	
Introduction and Variations on an Original Theme	82	1817	
	No. 2	1818	
Rondo, D major	138	1818	"Notre amitié est invariable" (? for Josef Gahy).
4 Polonaises	75	c. 1818	
Sonata, B Flat major	30	1818	Count Ferdinand Pálffy
Variations on a French Song (by Queen Hortense)	10	1818	
Overture, F major	34	1819	Beethoven

Title	Opus No.	Date composed	Dedication
Overture, G minor		1819	
3 'Marches héroïques'	27	before 1824	
'Divertissement à la hongroise'[1]	54	1824	Katharina Laczny
4 'Ländler'		1824	
Sonata, C major ("Grand Duo")[2]	140	1824	
Variations on an Original Theme, A Flat major	35	1824	Count Anton Berchtold
6 Marches	40	before 1825	J. Bernhardt
'Trauermarsch' for Tsar Alexander I	55	1825	Memory of Alexander I of Russia
6 Polonaises	61	c. 1825	
3 'Marches militaires'	51	before 1826	
'Divertissement en forme d'une marche brillante et raisonnée' on a French theme	63[3]	1826	

[1] First version of the Allegretto, the 'Ungarische Melodie' for flute solo (1824) published by O. E. Deutsch in 1928.
[2] Orchestrated by Joachim; sometime thought to be the lost 'Gastein' Symphony.
[3] Originally intended to be a part with Op. 84 Nos. 1 and 2 of one three-movement work, it was published separately.

Title	Opus No.	Date composed	Dedication
'Marche héroïque' for Tsar Nicholas I	66	1826	Nicholas I of Russia
2 'Marches caractéristiques'	121	1827 ? 1826	
'Andantino varié' on French themes	84 No. 1¹	1827	
Children's March, G major		1827	
'Rondo brillant' on French themes	84 No. 2¹	1827	
Variations on a theme from Hérold's 'Marie'	82 No. 1	1827	Kajetan Neuhaus
Fantasy, F minor	103	1828	Countess Karoline Esterházy
Fugue, E minor (see also Organ)	152	1828	
'Lebensstürme' (sonata movement)	144	1828	
Rondo, A major	107	1828	
Allegro moderato and Andante		?	

¹ See footnote 3 on facing page.

Recordings of all the main works, both solo and duet, are now available, as also are a few minor works.

APPENDIX II

BIBLIOGRAPHY

O. E. DEUTSCH AND D. R. WAKELING. *Schubert Thematic Catalogue* (Dent 1951); *Schubert: A Documentary Biography* (Dent 1946).

MAURICE BROWN. *Schubert, A Critical Biography* (Macmillan 1958), this work includes fresh data and discussion on the piano works; *Schubert's Variations* (Macmillan 1954).

KATHLEEN DALE. (in *Schubert, A Symposium* edited by Gerald Abraham OUP 1952). 'The Piano Works'—The most important essay in this country dealing with the works as a whole.

DONALD TOVEY. *Essays and Lectures on Music* (OUP 1949), discusses Schubert's form, especially the Sonata in B flat; *Essays in Musical Analysis*: Vol. I (OUP 1935), the Grand Duo as orchestrated by Joachim.

ALFRED EINSTEIN. *Schubert* (Cassell 1951).

ARTHUR HUTCHINGS. *Schubert* (Master Musicians Series 3rd ed. Dent 1956).

HEINRICH KREISSLE VON HELLBORN. *The Life of Franz Schubert* (Longmans 1869).

INDEX

171